Eastern Europe by Rail

Eastern Europe by Rail

Rob Dodson

BRADT PUBLICATIONS
THE GLOBE PEQUOT PRESS

First published in 1994 by Bradt Publications, 41 Nortoft Road, Chalfont St Peter, Bucks SL9 0LA, England and The Globe Pequot Press, Inc, 6 Business Park Rd, PO Box 833, Old Saybrook, Connecticut 06475-0833, USA.

British Library Cataloguing in Publication data
A catalogue record for this book is available from the British Library
ISBN 0 946983 95 X

Library of Congress Cataloging in Publication data
A catalogue record for this book is available from the Library of Congress
ISBN 1-56440-534-6

The author and publishers have made every effort to ensure the accuracy of the information in this book at the time of going to press. However, they cannot accept any responsibility for any loss, injury or inconvenience resulting from the use of information contained in this guide.

Rail maps taken from the *Thomas Cook New Rail Map of Europe*. © Thomas Cook Group Limited 1994.
Station maps by Patti Taylor.
Cover photos: Front, Steam locomotives at Mägdesprung in the Harz mountains, E. Germany, by Anthony Lambert. Back, courtesy German Railways.
Typeset from the author's disc by Patti Taylor, London NW10 1JR
Printed by The Guernsey Press Company Limited,
Guernsey, Channel Islands.

Acknowledgments

My thanks go to all those who have contributed to this book, especially Leon and Phoebe Spence, Annelie Müller, Angela and Peter of Schwallungen, Claudia Ruttman (Deutsche Reichsbahn), Odette Ortopan, Radu Cristescu, Svetoslav Stojanov, Ernst Fuchs and Brendan Fox with his team on the Thomas Cook European Timetable. Thanks also to Adrian Swash and Vera Poynton for their help, and to Sue Marbrow, who conscientiously produced successive drafts of the manuscript.

Thanks too to my contributors and updaters, Stephen Baister and Chris Patrick, Tim Burford, and Anthony Lambert.

Any errors of fact or interpretation are entirely my own. Whilst every effort has been made to ensure that information contained within this book was accurate at the time of going to press, changes inevitably occur. Readers' information, comments and suggestions are especially welcomed by me c/o Bradt Publications.

The Author

Rob Dodson spent his early years working on a farm followed by jobs in hotels, travel and as a diplomat and administrator. Since 1983, he has been teaching and writing in Europe and Asia. He has jointly edited two tourism textbooks in India and is currently completing a reader for Thai tourism students. He is an associate editor of the *International Journal of Management and Tourism,* a director of the Ost West Institute and a member of the Tourism Society of the UK.

Dedication

This book is dedicated to Eileen, Bert and Jane, who have supported me throughout and to Sam and Ben, who will soon be old enough to become independent rail travellers.

CONTENTS

ORDER FORM
European Rail Passes
(Effective Jan. 1, 1994 - Dec. 31, 1994)

EURAIL PASS (17 Countries) 1st Class

☐ 15 Days $498   ☐ 2 Months $1,098
☐ 21 Days $648   ☐ 3 Months $1,398
☐ 1 Month $798

EURAIL FLEXIPASS – 1st Class

☐ 5 Days in 2 Months $348
☐ 10 Days in 2 Months $560
☐ 15 Days in 2 Months $740

EURAIL SAVERPASS – 1st Class

☐ 15 Days $430   ☐ 1 Month $678
☐ 21 Days $550

Price is per person / 3 people must travel together at all times. (Two people may travel between Oct. 1st and March 31st)

EURAIL YOUTHPASS* – 2nd Class

☐ 15 Days $398   ☐ 2 Months $768
☐ 1 Month $578

EURAIL YOUTH FLEXIPASS* – 2nd Class

☐ 5 Days in 2 Months $255
☐ 10 Days in 2 Months $398
☐ 15 Days in 2 Months $540

*Pass holder must be under age 26 on first day of use.

EURAIL DRIVE PASS

There is an excellent Rail/Drive program that combines a Eurail Pass with Hertz or Avis Rent-a-Car. Call us for a comprehensive brochure.

EUROPASS (5 Countries)
France / Germany / Italy / Switzerland / Spain

3 COUNTRIES EUROPASS – 1st Class

☐ 5 Days in 2 Months $280
☐ 6 Days in 2 Months $318
☐ 7 Days in 2 Months $356

4 COUNTRIES EUROPASS – 1st Class

☐ 8 Days in 2 Months $394
☐ 9 Days in 2 Months $432
☐ 10 Days in 2 Months $470

5 COUNTRIES EUROPASS – 1st Class

☐ 11 Days in 2 Months $508
☐ 12 Days in 2 Months $546
☐ 13 Days in 2 Months $584
☐ 14 Days in 2 Months $622
☐ 15 Days in 2 Months $660

Note: You must specify the countries when ordering and the countries must border each other, e.g. Spain/France/Italy.

EUROPASS ASSOCIATE COUNTRIES

These countries may be added to any EuroPass for a flat charge per country. They expand the geographic scope of the pass, not the length.

☐ Austria $35   ☐ Portugal $22
☐ Belgium & Luxembourg $22

Youth rates – All EuroPasses are available for persons under age 26 in 2nd class at substantial discounts. Call!

(Continued on next page)

POINT-TO-POINT TICKETS, SLEEPERS, RESERVATIONS, GROUP RATES (10 or more, 25 or more) – we can help you with all of these. Call for rates.

For Travelers from North America
CALL TOLL FREE 1-800-367-7984
(Charge to Visa, Discover or MasterCard)

Forsyth Travel Library, Inc.
9154 W. 57th, P.O. Box 2975 • Shawnee Mission, KS 66201-1375

Forsyth Travel Library, Inc., is the leading agent in North America for the European and British Railroads and distributor of the famous Thomas Cook European Timetable. We are international rail travel specialist. Members: ASTA, Better Business Bureau of Kansas City, MO and International Map Trades Association. Free catalogs upon request listing all rail passes, timetables, accessories and maps. Official membership agency for American Youth Hostels/International Hostelling.

All prices shown are US Dollars – prices in effect July 1, 1994 – December 31, 1994

Section 1

Planning and Preparations

Chapter 1

INTRODUCTION

For so long virtually out of bounds for the independent traveller, the former Soviet satellite states have held a Cinderella status for the Western tourist. Short breaks now advertised to Prague, Warsaw, Berlin or Budapest demonstrate the cultural and historical attraction of these centres. You can now travel by train from the Baltic to the Black Sea and view landscape which has changed little over the years.

There are two immediately obvious advantages to travelling by rail: the new experience which includes people and places, and the unquestionable fact that it is cheap.

From an eastern European perspective, no guilt should be involved in relation to cost because it is recognised that income from tourists is extremely welcome. Above this, you will be impressed with the friendliness and hospitality. Service is another matter. Years of state control have fostered a working philosphy best summed up as 'the state pretends to pay me and I pretend to work'. Patience is a virtue you may need to acquire as simple transactions can take time.

Incomes are lower so many people do not own a car and, therefore, travel by train. It is not unusual for food and drink to be shared and addresses exchanged on the journey. With the collapse of communism, eastern European people are keen to meet Westerners and learn more about the market economy and life in the West, generally.

The Countries

It is certain that political, economic and social change will continue in eastern Europe. It will not be at the same rate, so we cannot look at the countries in a homogeneous way.

Economically, there has been a split between the wealthier and more industrialised north and the poorer south. Eastern Germany, now part of the unified state of Germany, is expected to develop more rapidly. Poland, the Czech Republic, Slovakia and Hungary have a strong economic base, although the agricultural sector appears less advanced than our own. The southern states of Romania and Bulgaria are viewed, even by their neighbours, as weak. It is here that you will observe horse-driven transport in the rural areas. It is also here that there may be less choice of food in all but the most luxurious places. Do not expect every amenity that you take for granted at home. Shortages and distribution problems are still in evidence, but there are many compensations.

Rail Travel

Travel by rail really does have the edge on other modes of transport for long distance sightseeing in eastern Europe. A glance at any road atlas will confirm very limited motorway provision. Progress on other roads can be erratic, given poor road surfaces and other obstructions. The choice of train travel is, therefore, very practical. The network is extensive and this book covers many of the main routes linking centres which you may wish to visit. It also estimates the shortest time for rail travel between centres. Only where rail travel is inappropriate or impossible are alternatives suggested. Generally, you will find that your choice to travel this way will not be disappointing and that so much is accessible. Station services, too, are surprisingly extensive. Often quite small stations will have a buffet and a luggage office. Staff are invariably courteous and, on one occasion, whilst waiting for some time I was invited to share the warmth of a Romanian station master's office. Tea and melon were proffered and a cordial discussion took place, during which a friend, waiting for me in Constanţa, was notified of the delay.

Gateways to Eastern Europe

Your choice of gateway depends, partly, on whether you wish to arrive by rail or air.

Air transport to any of the capitals is good value from the West at present, but you should choose one with good rail links such as Berlin, Warsaw, Prague, Budapest, Vienna and Sofia. Public transport usually connects airport and city centre every 30 minutes or less. The *Thomas Cook European Timetable* and their *Airports Guide Europe* give further details.

Rail travellers from western Europe can obviously choose from a wider range of destinations but some centres are better placed for both long distance rail travel and local excursions. International expresses link most of the major cities in eastern Europe but Berlin and Vienna are exceptionally good points to begin eastwards rail travel from Western countries.

Berlin

At a crossroads, for heading to all four points of the compass, international trains from here provide regular services linking the eastern capitals. Berlin has good links with western Europe as well. Two international express trains leave London daily. Refer to the section on Berlin for greater detail.

Vienna

The capital of Austria, historically closely linked with eastern Europe, is a traditional gateway. The former Hapsburg Empire at times embraced all of Austria, Hungary, Slovakia and Croatia, and parts of present day Romania, the Czech Republic, Poland and Ukraine. It is not intended to expand on the city but a short section below will assist should you wish to stop here on your way.

There is a direct daily rail service (overnight) to Vienna from London arriving around 1100. The return journey currently leaves early evening arriving early afternoon in London.

Vienna has direct links with Prague, Warsaw, Budapest, Bucharest and Sofia. It also has a number of railway stations (clarification on the destinations from these is given in the Vienna boxes).

Vienna Franz Josef

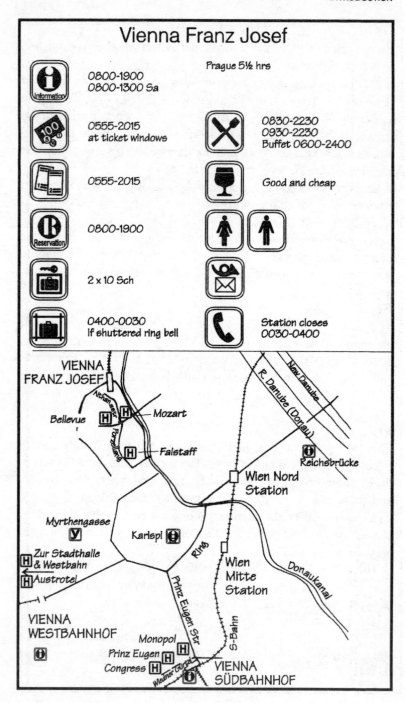

Prague 5½ hrs

0800-1900
0800-1300 Sa

0555-2015
at ticket windows

0830-2230
0930-2230
Buffet 0600-2400

0555-2015

Good and cheap

0800-1900

2 x 10 Sch

0400-0030
If shuttered ring bell

Station closes
0030-0400

Vienna Südbahnhof

 0630-2120

Warsaw 8¼ hrs, Kraków 8 hrs,
Budapest 2¾ hrs, Venice 8 hrs,
Prague 5 hrs, Bratislava 1¼ hrs
Lost and Found Buro 0700-1700 M-F

 0630-2100
(summer 2200)

 0600-2300

 0430-2400

 As above

 2 x 10 Sch

 24hrs

 0400-2400

 Station closes
0110-0400

Vienna Westbahnhof

 0630-2100

Budapest 3½ hrs, Munich 4½ hrs,
Cologne 10 hrs, Paris 12 hrs,
Sofia 19 hrs, Bucharest 19½ hrs

 0700-2200
also automatic
change machine

 0600-2300

 0400-0100

 2 x 10 Sch

 0400-0115

 Station closes
0115-0400

Tourist Information
Main Office Vienna, Kärnter Straße 1, just north of Karlsplatz, daily 0900-1900. Also at Südbahnhof 0630-2200 and Westbahnhof, 0615-2300.

Accommodation
Upper range
Hotel Prinz Engen, Wiedner Gürtel 14 (tel 505 1741) singles from AS915 to AS1495, doubles from AS1450 to AS2200 en suite with breakfast, near Südbhanhof.

Hotel Bellevue, Althanstraße 5 (tel 31348), sister hotel with same rates as Prinz Eugen, close to Franz Josef Bahnhof. Triples are available here AS1850 to AS2600.

Middle range
Hotel Congress, Wiedner Gürtel 34-36 (tel 505 9165/505 5506), single AS890, double AS1390, triple AS1640 inclusive with breakfast.

Hotel Mozart, Nordbergstraße, singles all AS750, doubles AS1300 including breakfast, bath/shower. Near Westbahnhof.

Hotel Westbahn, Pelzgasse 1 (tel 982 1480) singles from AS880, doubles from AS1230. Near Westbahnhof.

Budget
Pension Zur Stadthalle, Hackengasse 20 (tel 982 4272), singles from AS510, doubles from AS710 with showers extra, breakfast included. Close to Westbahnhof.

Pension Monopol, Prinz Eugen Straße 68, singles from AS210, doubles from AS780.

Pension Falstaff, Müllnergasse 5 (tel 349127), singles from AS345 without shower, AS465 with shower, doubles from AS565 inclusive of breakfast.

Hostel
Myrthengasse Youth Hostel, Myrthengasse 7 (tel 936316) AS140 for IYHF/YHA members, AS180 non members.

The City Hostel is now closed.

Budapest

The city is located centrally within eastern Europe and it is easy to travel either north or south. Many international expresses stop here. Accommodation is expensive for the east but modest by Western standards. You also begin your travels in a distinctly eastern place. (See the Budapest section in Chapter 6.)

At the time of writing, there are no direct international expresses to Budapest from London but you can take the express to Vienna Westbahnhof, and there will be a further three hours journey, leaving from the same station.

PLANNING YOUR TRIP

Preliminaries

Having made the decision to travel in eastern Europe, it is important to obtain the necessary documents. This can take time.

Passports

A full 10-year passport is required for all the countries in this book, at the time of writing, with the exception of **eastern Germany**. As it is part of the Federal Republic of Germany and, therefore, the European Union, EU regulations permit UK and Union citizens to use a one year passport or identity card.

Visas

Visas are no longer required for the **Czech Republic**, **Hungary**, **Poland** or the **Slovak Republic**, by nationals of the UK, many European countries and North America. Visas are required for both **Bulgaria** and **Romania**. For **Bulgaria**, obtain an application form in person, or by post sending a self addressed envelope. These are valid for three months from the date of issue and are issued seven working days after the date of application. For **Romania**, no form is required; send

(a)   Valid, 10-year passport;
(b)   Letter outlining intended itinerary and purpose of visit;
(c)   Passport photo.

Visas and further particulars are available from:

Bulgarian Embassy, Consular Section, 188 Queensgate, London
SW7 5HL (tel. 071 584 9400), £20 single entry.
Romanian Embassy, 4 Palace Green, London W8 (tel 071 937
9666). The addresses of embassies and national tourist offices can
be found at the back under *Useful Addresses*. £21, or £26 for
same-day service. Cheques are not accepted.

Maps and References

Whilst this book will assist you in deciding where you wish to
go, part of the enjoyment of travelling is at the planning stage.
This too, can be done whilst you are waiting for your visas to
arrive or waiting for information from the tourist organisations.
No serious rail traveller in Europe should be without the *Thomas
Cook European Timetable*. This includes rail maps, rail service
timetables, major ferry and hydrofoil routes, airport links and city
centre station location maps. There is also a companion map *The
Thomas Cook New Rail Map of Europe* which is excellent for
plotting the more scenic routes by rail. The recently published
Thomas Cook European Rail Travellers Phrase Book came out
too late for me to use this time. It is a handy pocket book of
useful phrases which will make you more independent, in many
European languages. In eastern Europe, the French, German,
Czech and Polish will be useful but the inclusion of Bulgarian is
especially welcome. It is now being tested by Richard Marbrow
and Matthew Adey, who will report for the next edition of
Eastern Europe by Rail. Available through Thomas Cook Retail
Shops, good bookshops and by mail order from Thomas Cook
Publishing (TPO/FE), PO Box 227, Peterborough PE3 6SB, UK,
and Forsyth Travel Library Inc, 9154 West 57th Street, PO Box
2975, Dept TCT, Shawnee Mission, Kansas 66201, USA.

Maps of eastern Europe are available from good bookshops.
Not all include rail routes. Ideally, it is useful, therefore, to have
one which covers at least the major railways with clear outlines
of the physical terrain. Stanfords, the famous London map and
travel shop at 12-14 Long Acre, London WC2E 9PL, have
maximum choice. They also provide a mail order service — tel
071 836 1321.

Free maps and lots of additional information are available from the National Tourist Office of the respective country (see under *Useful Addresses*). When you write to them, do specify what you would like and send a large SAE. Otherwise, they are likely to send you their latest package deal brochure.

On your map, mark the places you wish to visit so that you can decide the most convenient point of entry/gateway. With the European timetable you can also decide whether a route is feasible within your time scale.

By this time, you may well have obtained some of the more detailed guides (see Appendix for a selected list of guidebooks). One, which covers the world and is widely used by travel agents, is the *World Travel Guide* (Columbus Press), published annually. It is available in some libraries and has a section on every country of the world. The sections provide a basic breakdown of tourist attractions as an initial point of reference. They also give lots of basic useful information for the traveller but the guide is too bulky and wide ranging to travel with.

How long

The length of your stay will, obviously, depend on personal preference but, to begin to exploit this rail network, a minimum of two weeks is desirable. One month is better, as it gives you the opportunity to sample most of eastern Europe fairly rapidly.

Two week and one month periods give you the opportunity of saving time and money by purchasing one of the many passes now available to travellers. You no longer need to be a student, under 26 or a resident outside Europe to qualify for these bargains.

CONTINENTAL RAIL AND RAIL PASSES

Rail pass availability and coverage is subject to change, so it is best to deal with the specialists. A centralised information and booking service is provided by the International Rail Centre, Victoria Station, London SW1 1JY, phone 071 834 2345 (enquiries) or 071 828 0892 (credit card bookings). You can also contact British Rail International at selected stations or through their appointed agents in most towns in the UK. Phone the

London number for the name and phone number of your nearest agent.

Inter-Rail

In the early 1990s, changes in eastern Europe had put the future of the Inter-Rail pass in doubt, but the 1994 season brought some good news: media pressure together with the involvement of the Council of Europe brought recognition that Inter-Railing was good for Europe. This should put the scheme on a firmer footing.

This pass is valid for second class travel in all eastern European countries as well as those in western Europe. To qualify, you need to have been resident in Great Britain or Northern Ireland for at least six months and hold a valid passport. Take your passport when you buy your pass.

Inter-Rail for the under 26s costs up to £249 and is valid for up to 26 countries in a zonal system. Whilst all countries featured here fall into one zone, eastern Germany and Vienna fall into a second zone and unfortunately principal ferry entry ports in France, Belgium and Holland into a third. Finding the best value may not be straightforward but British Rail International can advise. To minimise hassle it may be prudent to purchase a pass for additional zone(s) rather than a transit return ticket.

Zone prices are as follows:

Any 1 Zone	£179	for 15 days
Any 2 Zones	£209	for 1 month
Any 3 Zones	£229	for 1 month

In 1991, Inter-Rail introduced a similar scheme for travellers over 26, entitled Inter-Rail 26+. There are two passes on offer in 1994 and both include all of the eastern European countries featured here.

Inter-Rail 26+ 15 days £209

Inter-Rail 26+ 1 month £269

The two passes are not valid on British Rail or on cross-channel services between Britain and the countries of Europe in the scheme. However, discounted travel is available from the UK to Germany and the Netherlands, where the pass is valid.

Rail Europe Senior

For those over 60 who hold a British Rail Senior Card, the Rail Europe Senior Card is available at a cost of £5. This card is valid for one year and gives 30% discount on all international journeys including eastern Germany, the Czech Republic, Slovakia and Hungary.

Freedom Pass

This gives a choice of travel on any 3, 5 or 10 days within a one month period. Passes are available First Class, Second Class or Youth.

The above passes: Inter-Rail, Rail Europe Senior, and Freedom are all available through the International Rail Centre, Victoria. Those listed below are not.

Eurail

Eurail tickets may be bought from travel agents outside Europe and North Africa, by residents of those areas. They are broadly the equivalent of Inter-Rail.

For further information on passes available in the USA, phone the Forsyth Travel Library (toll free 1-800 367 7984).

Eurotrain

This company specialises in discount rail fares for under 26s, students of any age with an ISIC card, teachers and academics accompanying spouses and children. Tickets are valid for two months, on the explorer fares where you can stay for as long as you wish, anywhere on your chosen route. For eastern Europe, the Eastern Explorer is good value, as for £190 (1993) you would be able to visit London-Amsterdam-Berlin-Prague-Budapest, returning via Vienna and Brussels.

Special rail passes are also available for periods of unlimited rail travel in certain eastern countries, which are also valid for over 26s.

Full details are available from: Eurotrain, 52 Grosvenor Gardens, London SW1W 0AG (tel 071 730 3402). Tickets are also available from student travel shops including many STA and Campus Travel branches.

Wasteels

Wasteels Travel offer help in planning your trip, tailor-made packages including rail travel from London, hotel accommodation and train reservations in Europe; 121 Wilton Road, London, SW1V 1JZ (tel 071 834-7066).

They have offices throughout Europe and offer standard rail fare discounts for those under 26 years.

Ffestiniog Travel

This company is the travel 'wing' of the Ffestiniog Railway in Wales, established 1836. A member of the Continental Rail Agents Consortium, they have the experience to assist with any enquiries, backed up by an efficient ticket, reservations and pass service. Most of their business is by post.

They also offer escorted or unescorted rail package holidays to eastern European capitals (Prague and Budapest) and elsewhere. Ffestiniog Travel is at Harbour Station, Porthmadog, Gwynedd LL49 9NP (tel 0766 512340).

Country Passes

You may wish to consider purchasing passes as required within each eastern European country on arrival. This could allow more flexibility in terms of purchasing later and also the freedom to stay within one country longer. Passes for individual countires known as Freedom Passes can be purchased in the UK for Youth, First and Second Classes for periods of 3, 5 and 10 days. Up to date information is available from British Rail International Rail Centre, Victoria Station, London SW1V 1JY (tel 071 834 2345), selected stations and BRI appointed travel agents.

LUGGAGE

What you take with you is largely a matter of personal preference but travelling light on rail is a distinct advantage. Not only is your luggage easier to carry but it is easier to store on and off the train.

I feel the most practical piece of luggage for rail travel is the rucksack. Good ones are hardwearing with many pockets (some hidden) and an internal frame. They are comfortable to carry and strong, if selected carefully. I try to travel light with a 35 litre rucksack but 45 litres should be sufficient for those with more possessions. One disadvantage of using a rucksack is security, a problem that is difficult for any traveller to solve other than by being vigilant. You can also use padlocks and a length of chain for extra security. A good strong money belt which goes around your waist underneath clothing should protect small valuable items like currency, travellers cheques and passport.

HEALTH

All countries have reciprocal medical arrangements with the UK and other members of the European Union; however, appropriate insurance is desirable. Prescribed medicines must be paid for so it may be advisable to take a stock with you.

MONEY

Only eastern Germany uses hard currency. You will, therefore, need to change money to obtain local currency at the border or within the country. If you are travelling extensively, it is useful to have low denomination notes in Deutschmarks, sterling and US dollars. Generally, Deutschmarks are the most versatile but, in some countries, for example Romania, the US dollar is king. Remember to keep your receipts for converting back to hard currency at the frontier.

Travellers Cheques

It is unwise to keep all your money in cash. £50 will go a long way when backpacking and sleeping on the trains. Travellers cheques, again in smaller denominations, are better. If they are stolen, they can be reimbursed through appropriate channels within the country. Travellers cheques can be exchanged at some banks, hotels and tourist information offices. Large railway stations also have exchange facilities. Opening times are indicated in the station information boxes in this book.

Credit Cards

These are another source of cash if required. Most cards are acceptable but the better known ones such as Visa and Mastercard are the most widely recognised and accepted by larger hotels and restaurants. In country areas, you will find that cash is almost exclusively used.

Informal Exchange

With inflation far higher than in the west, you may be approached to change money on the black market. This can occur at railway stations in particular. In most cases the gain to you will be minimal, while the loss could be quite high if the 'exchanger' chooses to substitute forged or worthless notes. In certain countries, you might wish to use hard currency to pay for accommodation in a private house. This will be welcomed and is legal in the Czech and Slovak republics for example, where room rates are sometimes given in DM. You may also wish to carry small gifts from home for special friends as an expression of thanks.

Steam in Eastern Germany

by Anthony Lambert

Because reunification of the former East and West Germanies was so recent, there remains a marked difference between the nature of steam workings on offer in the two areas. The relative affluence of the West meant that an interest in steam locomotives could be more easily translated into preservation, whether of locomotives based at museum depots that worked excursions over the lines of Deutsche Bundesbahn, or into preserved lines.

In East Germany steam survived on both standard and narrow gauge lines for much longer, the former lingering into the early 1990s and narrow gauge steam surviving reunification on most of the few remaining 75cm, 90cm or metre gauge lines. The state ensured that a good number of standard gauge steam locomotives was saved. These run on specials over German Railways lines, often as part of imaginatively organised Plandampfs, which are weekend or week-long festivals of steam. Sometimes, even commercial freight trains are worked by steam during such events.

For the narrow gauge lines, reunification came at just the right time. In early 1973 it was reported that such railways would probably be extinct by 1975, except for one unspecified line that was to be kept as a tourist attraction. Thankfully this threat was never carried out, but plans were drawn up to replace steam on the busiest lines. This was to be achieved in part by converting surplus standard gauge diesels to metre gauge, and the first arrived in the Harz mountains in February 1989.

It is probable, if unverifiable, that the attitude in the reunified Germany was more favourably disposed towards the retention of steam than would have been the case under Communism. The outcome has been pressure to retain steam as a tourist attraction on all the remaining lines, although it should not be forgotten that they all continue to serve an important local transport function, carrying passengers and/or freight. They are therefore not preserved railways, although some special trains are run for the benefit of enthusiasts and tourists.

As a result of their continued role serving local communities, these narrow gauge railways have a character and atmosphere that is unique in Europe: no other country has such a collection of lines in different parts of the country, still operated by steam on a daily basis. They are, of course, only a fragment of what once existed. Before the Second World War there were 132 narrow gauge lines (excluding electric tramways) with a total length of 4,860 miles

Steam trains in Eastern Germany

(7776km). But the qualities that have attracted generations of travellers and connoisseurs of byways are still to be found.

The narrow gauge was chosen in the first place because the area to be served was insufficiently populous to support a standard gauge railway; this was especially true if close-set contours pushed up the costs of heavy engineering structures. Narrow gauge railways can cope with sharper radius curves to reduce the need for such works, but if they are unavoidable, there was a considerable saving by building bridges or tunnels to a narrower width and for lighter trains. Added to the intrinsic rural nature of such railways is the appeal of all narrow gauge railways, hard to convey to those who have yet to be exposed to their charm but bound up with their smallness. There is something about the modest size of the locomotives, rolling stock and even stations that imbues them with a fascination quite different from the sheer impressiveness of a standard gauge steam locomotive hard at work.

However, the best-known and most extensive of the east German narrow gauge systems is the one which least possesses this characteristic, on account of having the widest of the three narrow gauges — metre gauge. Not only do the steam locomotives look big enough to be standard gauge, but the diesels on the line are converted from the larger gauge. What are now called the Harzer Schmalspurbahn (HS) lines have undergone a renaissance during the 1990s, thanks to the reopening of closed lines and major overhauls of the massive steam locomotives. In part this is due to the attractiveness of the country in which the lines are set: within months of reunification a tourist organisation had been formed to promote the Harz mountains which straddled the old border.

Until 1984 these lines formed two separate networks, although they had once been linked: the Harzquerbahn ran north to south for 37 miles (60.5km) from Wernigerode to Nordhausen with branches off to Schierke and to Hasselfelde; and the Selketalbahn which commenced at Gernrode and went south for 9 miles (14 km) to Alexisbad, junction for the 2 mile (3.2km) branch to Harzgerode and the line that connected with the Harzquerbahn at Stiege. For many years the section between Strassberg and Stiege was closed, but the prospect of substantial coal traffic from Nordhausen to a power station at Silberhütte prompted reopening of the link for freight in 1983 and passengers the next year.

Today trains continue to operate between Wernigerode and Nordhausen, but the new service over the link runs between Gernrode and Eisfelder Talmühle. There are also separate Gernrode - Harzgerode and Stiege - Hasselfelde trains. These lines provides an 81 mile (130km) network through the heart of the Harz Mountains, for which a range of passes is available allowing unlimited travel.

These lines were constructed shortly before the turn of the century, in part to develop the tourist potential of the forests and gorges, but also to help with the extraction of minerals and timber. The first company to be formed, in 1886, was the Gernrode Harzgeroder Eisenbahngesellschaft (GHE), the first section opening the following year. A decade later construction was under way from both ends of the Nordhausen–Wernigeroder Eisenbahn (NWE), through services starting in 1899. The two systems were linked by the Südharzeisenbahn, the GHE having reached Stiege in 1891 and Hasselfelde the following year. In 1946 the GHE was completely dismantled and taken to the USSR as war reparations, so it had to be reconstructed, though the section beyond Strassberg was not relaid. The SHE was closed and demolished in 1963.

By rail, the most accessible places on the system are Nordhausen and Wernigerode, but the latter is the more attractive town to stay. Overshadowed by the multi-turreted castle of 1862, Wernigerode is a delightful town of half-timbered buildings beside pedestrianised streets. On the outskirts, adjacent to Westerntor station, is the works that carries out most of the repair work on the Harz lines rolling stock; locomotives are sent to Görlitz works right on the border with Poland. The railway keeps close company with the road, requiring frequent use of whistle and bell. A stiff climb at 1 in 30 takes the train through the only tunnel on east Germany's narrow gauge lines and up to the junction at Drei Annen Hohne. Here trains leave the main line for the branch up to one of Germany's most famous mountains, Brocken at 3747ft (1142m). The poet Heinrich Heine allowed his imagination free reign as he climbed the mountain, conjuring up visions related to the gathering of witches here on Walpurgis Night. It is also the setting for a scene in Goethe's Faust, perhaps inspired by his climb of the mountain when he was 28: 'I stood on the summit of the Brocken and between those ominous crags I cast my gaze over the endless snow. Beneath me I saw a motionless sea of cloud, the position of the surrounding mountains only indicated by the varying levels at which it had settled.'

The views from Brocken and its unique flora and fauna — largely the result of the area being on the border and so out of bounds for decades — now attracts huge numbers of visitors, making this one of the busiest sections of the HS. Moreover, this is one of the most exciting sections of the system. Until 1991 the line was abandoned beyond Schierke, but after complete rebuilding it was reopened to specials in September that year and to regular services from 1992. The line has a ruling gradient of 1 in 30, producing a stirring sound from the locomotive as it winds its way up the mountain to the final corkscrew loop to the open summit station. There are several trails through the nature reserve, but visitors are asked not to leave them.

One descends to Schierke, following the railway for much of the way.

Continuing south from the junction at Drei Annen Hohne, the line reaches the summit just beyond Elend, at 1827ft (557m). Running close to the former border, this stretch of line was considered so sensitive that it was not even shown on maps. From the winter and summer resort of Benneckenstein, once also an iron-mining town, the line descends all the way to Nordhausen. At Eisfelder Talmühle is the junction for trains to Hasselfelde and Gernrode. Dropping down through the wooded valley of the Bere, the train calls at Ilfeld, another summer resort and the first place to be served by the railway: the first section of the NWE from Nordhausen to Ilfeld opened in 1897.

As the railway leaves the woods for open pasture, it passes close to a grim memorial to the suspension of human decency during the Second World War: it was inside the mountain of Kohnstein that V1 and V2 rockets were produced in a 7-mile (11km) labyrinth of massive tunnels. Both tunnels and rockets were built by 60,000 prisoners who lived in nearby Camp Dora; 20,000 of them were worked to death or shot. After a recent threat to the entire mountain from a west German mining company — Kohnstein is almost pure gypsum — major works have been undertaken to safeguard the tunnels and area and prepare them for opening to the public.

The narrow gauge joins the standard gauge on the approach to Nordhausen, an industrial town with a metre gauge tram system.

Returning to Eisfelder Talmühle, trains for Gernrode head east, passing a stone quarry that may help to revive levels of freight traffic on the HS. A fearsome 1 in 27 climb through pine woods brings the train to a small halt in a clearing at Birkenmoor, patronised by walkers, before it continues to the junction for Hasselfelde at Stiege. The 3-mile branch to the former mining town of Hasselfelde affords fine views of the Brocken as it passes through open pasture towards the small town. At Stiege a turning loop was installed to enable coal trains to run through without reversing; this is now used by some passenger trains. A lake-side castle dating from 1202 makes a worthwhile reason to break the journey here.

From Stiege the railway climbs on to a plateau before diving again into forest and passing a reservoir at Mühlteich. It is worth leaving the train at Güntersberge to explore the delightfully sited town where there is a ruined castle on a nearby hill. The forest masks the site of a former fluospar mine on the way to Strassberg, situated beside the River Selke which once formed the boundary between Prussia and Anhalt. The railway continues to follow the river through undulating country, past the closed central boiler house at Silberhütte that prompted reopening of this section. There is still a sawmill and a fireworks factory which once provided the railway with traffic.

At the wooded junction of Alexisbad, a spa town, the choice can be made to continue north to Gernrode or change to travel the 2 mile (2.9km) branch to Harzgerode. This line climbs through more open views and past a lake to reach the terminus beside a sixteenth-century castle. Leaving Alexisbad, where the station has a buffet, the line takes on the character of a roadside tramway near Drahtzug Halt, paralleling the main road for some distance.

Mägdesprung was once the site of a large ironworks, founded by Prince Frederick Albert of Anhalt, who died in 1796. A comparison may be made with Ironbridge in Shropshire in that both early foundries produced 'tasteful articles in cast iron' as Baedeker described the products of Mägdesprung, which could be bought at the foundry by passing tourists. A hint of the former importance of the town is given by the size of the station, attractively sited on a curve.

There is quite a climb through open hills as the train leaves the scene of early industrial enterprise, the remains of the thirteenth-century Heinrichsburg Castle visible on a hill to the right. The summit is reached at Sternhaus-Ramberg, another station frequented by walkers. The former passing loop at Sternaus-Haberfeld, just beyond the last crossing of the main road as both road and rail begin the descent to Gernrode, is now a request stop.

Dropping down at grades of 1 in 30, the train skirts a couple of lakes and squeals down through orchards to reach the northern terminus at Gernrode, a town notable for its tenth-century Romanesque church with two round towers and the tomb of the town's founder, Margrave Gero, who died in 965.

The scenic delights of these lines would be worth enjoying from the most prosaic of railcars. In fact about half the trains are hauled by Europe's most powerful narrow gauge steam locomotives, the 65-ton 2-10-2 tank engines that can be found on most of east Germany's narrow gauge lines. Based on a design that dates from 1931, most were built between 1954 and 1956, although many of them have been substantially rebuilt at Görlitz works. New frames, boilers, cylinders, tanks, bunkers and boiler fittings have left only the axles, wheels and motion from the old locomotives. The HS also has eight vintage steam locomotives, three of which are Mallet 0-4-4-0Ts dating from 1897 which worked all trains on the Selketalbahn until the arrival of the 2-10-2Ts and diesels in the early 1980s. There is a unique 2-6-2T built by Krupp in 1939, a pair of rarely used 1914 Henschel 0-6-0Ts, and a Fairlie tram engine built by Hartmann. The Mallets are often used on what is now called the Oldtimerzug (formerly the Traditionzug).

The other narrow gauge lines are much less well known by

tourists but are none the less worth visiting, unless mountain scenery is the only motivation for travelling on the HS. Probably the busiest, and very popular with locals, is the 15 mile (24km) 75cm gauge line from Freital Hainsberg to Kurort Kipsdorf, near Dresden. Opened in 1882, the line passes through a wooded valley and skirts two large reservoirs, the station at Malter being popular with locals out for a swim or row. Five miles of steep gradients has the 2-10-2Ts barking away, and there is an attractive viaduct for photographs at Schmiedeberg, where a siding for loading scrap metal provides a source of freight. The size of the terminus at Kurort Kipsdorf is enormous with three long 'platforms' (narrow gauge lines seldom have such things) and refreshment room.

To the east of Dresden the town of Zittau is the starting point for another steeply graded line that runs south-west to Bertsdorf (5 1/2 miles, 9km); there a main line-sized signal-box — a rarity on the narrow gauge whatever the size — controls the junction for lines to the spa towns of Kurort Jonsdorf and Kurort Oybin, 2 1/2 miles (4km) and 2 miles (3km) respectively from Bertsdorf. ('Kurort' is German for spa.) Worked by pre-war 2-10-2Ts, the scenery at the Zittau end is unremarkable, but there is a fine curving stone viaduct at Olbersdorf. Beyond Bertsdorf the scenery on both lines is attractive, though the Oybin line is the more photogenic.

Just to the north west of Dresden on the main line to Berlin, and also on a tram line from Dresden, is the junction of Radebeul-Ost, from where a 75cm gauge line runs for 10 1/2 miles (17km) to Radeburg. The line climbs through a wooded valley before reaching a plateau with several lakes at Moritzburg. It is worth breaking the journey here, for the town has a fine museum which sheds fascinating light on the social life of Augustus the Strong, who used the nearby mansion as a shooting lodge where up to a hundred guests were entertained. His legacy was 352 children and many of the buildings admired today in Dresden, though they were built on the backs of punitive taxation and slave wages.

The scenery on to Radeburg is pleasant if unremarkable. The line is operated by post-war 2-10-2Ts, but the traditionzug is worked by either a 0-10-0T built in 1927 or a Saxon Meyer 0-4-4-0T in green livery with its old number, 132. Sometimes the staff wear Saxon State Railway costume and an open coach accommodates an 'oopah' band who, along with passengers, are kept supplied with beer from a bar car. A small museum in the goods shed at Radebeul provides an insight into the history of the Saxon narrow gauge railways.

Further west on the Dresden-Leipzig line, beyond Riesa is the town of Oschatz. Here a once-extensive network of 75cm gauge line connected with the main line; today it brings standard gauge wagons mounted on narrow gauge transporters (rollwagen) loaded with china clay from a works 10 miles (16km) away at Kemmlitz. This traffic has kept the line open, but there have long been fears that it will be lost to road, and worsen congestion; the passenger service was withdrawn years ago, although a traditionzug operates on certain weekends with coaches in chocolate with yellow lining. The line's great attraction for enthusiasts was that it had no locomotives other than the elderly Saxon-Meyer 0-4-4-0 tanks; however, the railway was privatised at the beginning of 1994, and the new company has introduced less powerful diesels on the freight workings.

To the south of Chemnitz (Karl Marx Stadt under the old order) is a 75cm gauge line that runs to the highest station on the railways of former East Germany, situated in the Obererz Mountains. Leaving the line served by standard gauge trains between Bärenstein and Flöha at Cranzahl, the 10 1/2 mile (17km) line climbs through rather bleak coniferous woods that bring to mind the melancholic paintings of Caspar David Friedrich. After about an hour's exertion and a brush with the Czech border, the 2-10-2T pulls into Kurort Oberwiesenthal station, at 2926ft (892m). Trains to this ski resort are well patronised, some of which are augmented by the use of a saloon car in Saxon Railways olive green and cream livery. A traditionzüge is operated during the summer, hauled by a pair of Saxon-Meyers.

A few miles to the north of Cranzahl are the remains of a line that closed a few years too soon to be saved by reunification. It is a particularly sad loss, as it was one of the most scenic. The 75cm line connected with the Cranzahl-Chemnitz line at Wolkenstein, close to the old lace-making town of Annaberg-Buchholz. The railway ran through glorious countryside to the small town of Jöhstadt and was for years rumoured to be on the point of closure, but a healthy traffic in refrigerators from a factory at Niederschmiedeberg kept it alive. It was also well patronised by ramblers, sometimes requiring two engines to work the long train. However, it closed in November 1986, and local enthusiasts were forbidden by the communist government to try to preserve it. The line was lifted and 30 of the 52 bridges gratuitously removed, in some cases using helicopters to remove the girders — at a cost far higher than the scrap value of the metal.

That would have been the end of the story but for reunification. Now, against all the odds, a group of enthusiasts is endeavouring to rebuild the railway. The engine shed at Jöhstadt is being rebuilt, and an entire train was found hidden in the middle of a wood, stranded when the bridges on either side were removed. The first goal is Schmalzgrube, 2½ miles (4km) from Jöhstadt, followed by Steinbach.

The last two lines are very distant from the others, in character as well as space. Both serve the Baltic coast and have long enjoyed a healthy tourist traffic as well as locals. Opened in 1886 as the Mecklenburgische Friedrich-Franz Eisenbahn, the 90cm gauge line from Bad Doberan, west of Rostock, runs for 9 1/2 miles (15.4km) to the seaside town of Ostseebad Kühlungsborn West. The railway is unusual in Germany in having a section that runs through the street and across a main square, like a tramway. In an extraordinary twist of logic, the street running sections have been under threat because of an increase in road traffic since reunification, and almost as incomprehensible is the opposition to the railway of some environmentalists. They object to the smoke (much less harmful than car emissions), but a survey of local residents revealed 90 per cent support for retaining the street running sections.

The line is operated by Orenstein & Koppel 2-8-2Ts to a design dating from 1932 and has a service of 14 trains daily in each direction. For photographers this compensates for the rather flat landscape, though the crossing point at Heiligendamm is in an attractive wooded setting. The station at Heiligendamm Steilküste is the choice for runpasts on the two trains a day that are billed as 'enthusiasts' trains'.

Finally the island of Rügen has a fragment of a once-extensive network of 75cm gauge lines. The island was made famous by being the subject of many paintings by Caspar David Friedrich, and although parts of the 15 1/4 mile (24.4km) railway from Putbus to Göhren are flat it climbs through pleasant woods for part of the way. The pre-First World War Baedeker records that beyond the station of Sellin, 'the railway...now enters the rugged peninsula of Mönchgut, where the primitive native customs and peculiar costume still prevail'. Putbus resembles an English south-coast resort with its rows of classical white-washed houses, though sadly the palace of its founder, Prince Malte, was pulled down after being badly damaged during the war. The railway enjoys a greater variety of motive power, trains being hauled by 2-10-2, 2-8-0 and 0-8-0 tank engines. A recent surprise was the decision to reboiler at Görlitz works the 0-8-0T, built in 1914 by Vulkan in Stettin for the Rügen Light Railway and always based on the railway. The 2-10-2Ts are not popular with crews who prefer the ex Kleinbahn des Kreises Jerichow 2-8-0Ts.

For those interested in miniature gauges, there are a number of Pioneer Railways operated by children. These are in part a legacy of the communist era during which such railways were promoted throughout the Soviet Union and its satellites to groom children for a railway career. In Dresden, for example, there is 2 mile (3.2km) 15in gauge line taking half an hour for the journey. Some trains are diesel-hauled, but others are worked by one of the two Krauss Pacifics of 1927. A third Krauss Pacific operates a similar line in

Leipzig. Not all are so small a gauge: the Pioneer Railway in Cottbus is 600mm with an 0-8-0T.

Summary

Wernigerode - Nordhausen, Gernrode - Hasselfelde (Harz mountains)

Freital Hainsberg - Kurort Kipsdorf

Zittau - Kurort Jonsdorf/Kurort Oybin

Radebeul Ost - Radeburg

Oschatz - Kemmlitz

Cranzahl - Kurort Oberwiesenthal

Bad Doberan - Ostseebad Kühlungsborn West

Putbus - Göhren

Preserved Steam in Eastern European Countries

It is no wonder that the countries of eastern Europe have nothing to rival the preserved railways of western Europe. Until they gained independence there was no freedom to develop a voluntary sector in which people could contribute their time and talents to preserve something to which they are committed. Lack of money remains a severe handicap, and the state remains the driving force behind many schemes to preserve steam locomotives.

This is particularly true in Poland where, in a remarkably innovative way, Polish railways (PKP) have simply kept steam locomotives working at a number of depots, operating both passenger and freight trains on a varying number of services. A nominal charge is usually made to visit the depots, at Wolsztyn, Koscierzyna and Chabówka. The country once had a large number of narrow gauge lines, most of which have been closed through the economic hardships that most of the former Soviet satellites have endured since independence. However, there are also narrow gauge museum operations at Znin and Sochaczew, and a museum in Pomerania at Gryfice where there remains 201 miles (323km) of a once much more extensive metre-gauge system.

Hungary and the Czech republic both have 760mm gauge preserved lines: in the former diesels work most trains on the lines from Kecskemét to Kiskunmajsa and Kiskorös, but an 0-8-0T works some excursions. In Czech the steadily expanding Hronec Forestry Railway was reopened as a museum operation in May 1992, running on the last Sunday in each month. Trains run up the Vydrovo valley from Cierny Balog.

Section 2

The Countries

The following seven chapters form a manual for the dedicated independent rail traveller. It is assumed that detailed tourist information will be obtained in advance or en route. Therefore, the briefest of introductory detail is provided to allow space for the immediate and essential information.

Each chapter has the capital city as the major entry. Boxes and maps prepare you for arrival at stations, so that you can obtain what you need in the shortest possible time. Details of tourist information, foreign currency and postal services (where they are not available in the station) are then listed.

It is assumed that your next pressing need is somewhere to stay. Some accommodation with price guide is given. This must be seen as *only a guide*. Inflation and the timespan between research and printing does not permit absolute accuracy. Hard currency in US dollars or Deutschmarks has been used to assist comparison. Every effort has been made to locate a range of accommodation close to stations.

Sightseeing is a matter of personal preference. In the capitals and resorts a selection of sights (by no means extensive) is included. Also in the capitals, a section on city transport/orientation is included to assist you to move around. Unfamiliar customs or payment procedures are also given.

Pronunciation and spelling differ widely from English and between the countries. Centres are spelt in the language of the host country with the exception of Bulgaria, which uses the Cyrillic script, where an anglicised spelling is given. An equivalent English spelling accompanies the first entry when this differs from the name you would recognise.

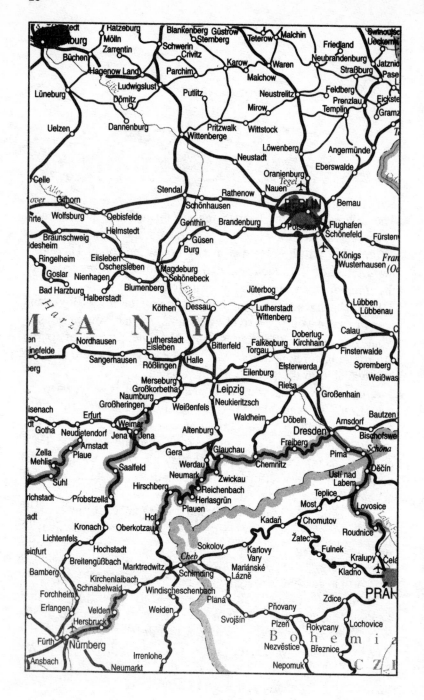

Chapter 2

Eastern Germany

with additional material by Stephen Baister and Chris Patrick

Area: 108,300 km² (41,600 sq miles) Population: 16,600,000
Capital Berlin Population (East and West) 3½m

INTRODUCTION

Eastern Germany is no longer a separate country but is included in this guide as the area of Germany that was formerly the German Democratic Republic (GDR) and as such was formerly part of eastern Europe, and because a rail journey to many parts of eastern Europe will still generally take the traveller through Berlin and eastern Germany.

After the defeat of Hitler's Reich in 1945 Germany was occupied by Soviet, US and British (later also French) forces. Tensions grew up between Stalin's Soviet Union and the Western occupiers, and Germany soon became the focus of those tensions. During 1948-49 Stalin blockaded the western sectors of Berlin (the four occupying powers each governed one sector of the wartime capital) in an attempt to force the West to abandon the city, but failed, defeated by the Berlin air lift of food and supplies to the western sectors. In 1949 the rift led to West Germany (under British, French and US occupation) forming the Federal Republic of Germany as a European state espousing liberal, democratic and firmly capitalist values, and East Germany proclaiming itself the German Democratic Republic, a communist state which, in the words of the GDR's 1974 constitution, was 'irrevocably allied with the Union of Soviet Socialist Republics'.

Disparities between the two regimes, in particular the standards of living in the two countries, eventually led to a decline in the population in the East, as Germans in the GDR left for the more prosperous West. The GDR government eventually acted by sealing the border between the two countries and beginning the erection (in August 1961) of what was to become the Berlin Wall. GDR citizens soon found themselves cut off from relatives and friends in the West and able to travel only in other communist states.

Relations between the GDR and the Federal Republic improved in the early 1970s, largely as a result of Willy Brandt's Ostpolitik which saw some rapprochement between the two German states. By 1987 the GDR's leader, Erich Honecker, felt able to accept an invitation from Chancellor Helmut Kohl to visit the Federal Republic. The two Germanies appeared destined to coexist peacefully, and although the Federal Republic still aspired, at least under the terms of its constitution (Grundgesetz), to a united Germany, nobody expected the two Germanies to become one again in the foreseeable future.

In autumn 1989 Hungary opened its borders to the West, and some 30,000 GDR citizens (who had access to Hungary) emigrated illegally to Austria. At the same time, political activists (in particular in Leipzig) began to demonstrate and to demand democratic reforms. The unrest grew and soon precipitated a political crisis in the GDR. Erich Honecker was deposed from office and replaced as head of state by Egon Krenz. In November 1989 president Gorbachev of the Soviet Union visited the GDR and made it clear to Krenz that he should undertake reforms and that the GDR could no longer look to the Soviet Union for support. In an attempt to placate the population, Krenz removed restrictions on travel between the GDR and the Federal Republic (perhaps the thing that had most irked people in the GDR). By the middle of November 1989 extensive openings had appeared in the Berlin Wall in addition to the official crossing points and it was clear that the GDR could no longer survive.

In September 1990 the Volkskammer (parliament) in East Berlin and the Bundestag in Bonn voted for the unification of Germany, and on October 3 1990 the two Germanies became one by what was in reality the incorporation of the GDR into the Federal Republic. Virtually all GDR institutions ceased to exist, and the former GDR became what are now known as 'die fünf neuen Bundesländer' — the five new Federal States.

But even if the two Germanies are now politically one, the differences between the West and the new Federal States is still clear to any traveller: the collapse of the communist state has brought about huge unemployment in the East and increased taxation for all German citizens to pay for the much needed development and reconstruction of the East. Even three years after unification, the infrastructure of the East remains in many respects primitive and the economy ailing.

RAILWAYS IN EASTERN GERMANY

The GDR boasted that it had the densest railway network in Europe, an average of 0.3km of track per square kilometre of land in the country as a whole and 1km of track per square kilometre in Berlin. Berlin, in spite of its division into East and West, was still the most significant railway junction city, and Leipzig, firmly in the GDR, had the largest passenger station in central Europe.

The division of Germany into the GDR and the Federal Republic meant that the two German states ran separate rail systems. By a quirk of history, the GDR kept on the Deutsche Reichsbahn (the prewar Imperial Railway) whilst West Germany renamed its railway the Deutsche Bundesbahn (the German Federal Railway). Even after unification the two rail networks have continued to operate side by side, although the elderly rolling stock and primitive track of the former GDR is gradually being replaced. The old East German railways had not seen significant investment for years; rail journeys were generally slow and far from luxurious, and trains frequently arrived late. High speed trains were unheard of.

In common with many countries, the German railway system is in a time of crisis. In spite of heavy subsidies the railways are set to cost the German taxpayers some DM570 billion over the next ten years. The response of the Federal government has taken the form of a plan to merge the Reichsbahn and the Bundesbahn and form out of them a new commercial company, Deutsche Bahn AG, with four divisions responsible for track, freight, passenger services and local services, each of which will become separate companies which can be privatised. At the same time the former monopoly has been lifted, and private companies now have access to the German track network, opening the railways up to competition for the first time.

A variety of trains operates in Germany as a whole, although not all the high speed services have yet reached the East. The most prestigious train type is the high speed ICE InterCityExpress (German tends to run words together rather than separate them as we do in English), a high-speed, modern and very comfortable train launched in 1991 which travels at speeds of up to 250km per hour. Carriage seats have aircraft-style radio channels and some seats have two video channels. Special fares apply. EC (EuroCity) and IC (InterCity) trains form the next significant category. InterCity trains run between the major German towns and cities, whilst the EuroCity trains connect the major German cities with other European centres such as Copenhagen, Warsaw, Prague, Brussels, Paris, Vienna and Budapest, and therefore do run through the East. ICE, EC and IC trains have restaurant cars and telephones. IR (InterRegio) trains provide the next category of service. IR trains run throughout East and West at up to 200km per hour in the West and up to 160km per hour in the East stopping at stations at intervals of about every 30km. They generally have a buffet car (BordTreff). Other types of train which you will encounter (in descending order of speed and importance) are the Schnellzug (express) designated by the letter D, RegionalSchnellBahn (regional express) RSB, Eilzug (fast train), designated by the letter E, and the suburban Citybahn. In major towns and cities the underground (U-Bahn) and overground trains (S-Bahn) provide cheap and efficient alternatives to buses.

The majority of trains are now very modern, but some of the trains and rolling stock found in the East are still old-fashioned, especially those coming from Russia or Poland and running on some of the narrow gauge rail systems that still operate. Watch out for the unusual double-decker trains that are found especially in the East.

For anyone interested in historical or unusual railways, many of which are still in genuine everyday use and not just there for tourists, eastern Germany offers many attractions (see *Steam in Eastern Germany*). Of particular interest are the Harz-Querbahn which runs between Nordhausen and Wernigerode or Quedlinburg (in the Harz area), and the Molli railway, which runs between Bad Doberan and Kühlungsborn (in the north). Other popular narrow gauge railways are the Erzgebirgsbahn (Cranzahl to Oberwiesenthal) and the Osterzgebirgsbahn (Freital-Hainsberg to Kipsdorf). In the woods of Thuringia the Deutsche Reichsbahn runs the steepest funicular railway in the world; the Thuringian Waldbahn (forest railway), in the same area, is not really a railway at all but a tram system.

Nostalgic rail travel has seen something of a revival in the East in recent years. Especially interesting are the steam trains that run between Berlin and Kaliningrad (the former German city of Königsberg lost to the USSR after the Second World War). The journey lasts about 14 hours. Occasional steam trips also take place in the form of the Elbflorenz Express (Berlin/Dresden) and the Spree-Elbe Express (Berlin/Hamburg). (Information and bookings from an office in the gallery of Berlin Hauptbahnhof or through Mochel-Reisen, 77933 Lahr/Schwarzwald, Georg-Vogel-Straße 2 (tel 07821 43037). Nostalgic rail excursions also operate in the Halle, Leipzig and Dresden areas. Further information can be obtained from the German publication, *Kursbuch der Deutschen Museums-Eisenbahnen* (available from Thomas Cook Publishing, P.O. Box 227, Peterborough PE3 6SB) or by contacting Deutsche Reichsbahn, Direktion Dresden, Ammonstraße 8, O-1069 Dresden. Other useful contact addresses for the rail enthusiast are Deutsche Gesellschaft für Eisenbahngeschichte eV (the German Society for Railway History), Post Box 11 11, 4714 Selm, Verein Sächsischer Eisenbahnfreunde e.V. (Saxon Railway Enthusiasts Club), Post Box 48, O-8028 Dresden. There is a good bookshop for rail enthusiasts in Leipzig station and another in Goethe-Straße, also in Leipzig.

Tickets and Rail Passes

Different fare rates apply depending on whether you are travelling on the Bundesbahn or the Reichsbahn. The rate that generally applies for a rail journey of any real length (ie over 101km) is 24 Pfennig per kilometre 2nd class and 36 Pfennig per kilometre 1st class on the Bundesbahn and 15 Pfennig 2nd class and 23 Pfennig 1st class on the Reichsbahn. A supplement (Zuschlag) is generally payable if you travel on InterRegio, Fern-Express (long distance express) or Schnellzug trains, and also on EuroCity or InterCity trains (although in these cases it is usually included in the reservation price).

You can save money by buying an annual BahnCard (rail card) that enables you to buy tickets at half price or by travelling in a group of more than six. Foreign travellers can also buy a German Rail Pass, a German Rail Twin Pass (available for any two people travelling together) or a German Rail Youth Pass (2nd class only, for young people aged 12-25). These can be purchased for periods of 5 days, 10 days or 15 days. Price details are available in the leaflet *German Rail Pass Discover Germany by Train*, available from stations or from specialist travel agents (such as DER, 18 Conduit Street, London W1R 9TD; tel: 071 408 0111).

Other Rail Information

Times of trains can be found in the German railway timetable, called the Kursbuch. Individual regional timetables (entitled Städteverbindungen or Fahrplan-Mitteilungsblatt) are available at stations free of charge. On platforms and in the subways connecting them or on the station concourse you will also generally find timetables giving details of departures and arrivals from that station. Be careful to distinguish between timetables for train departures (Abfahrt) and arrivals (Ankunft).

Many of the stations in eastern Germany have now been modernised and contain a travel centre (Reisezentrum) where you buy tickets, make reservations and where you can also obtain information on train times.

If you have a reservation it will be important to get into the correct carriage when your train arrives. For this reason, for any long distance train, you will generally find on the relevant platform a diagram of the make-up of your train called the Wagenstandanzeiger which you should consult so as to know where to stand on the platform before your train arrives. Trains do not always stop for long, even at major stations, and many trains crossing Germany or Europe can be exceptionally long and may divide en route.

At most important stations you will be able to leave your luggage in lockers (Schließfächer) or at the left luggage office (Gepäckaufbewahrung). You can also generally find luggage trollies (Kofferkulis) to help you move your luggage around in the station. Porters (Gepäckträger) are rare and generally have to be booked in advance to meet your train. At Berlin Zoo and the Hauptbahnhof there are lifts to take wheel chairs up to platform level. In the smaller stations, facilities for disabled travellers are limited.

There are a few words which are useful to know when buying a train ticket: single (einfach), return (hin und zurück), first class (erste Klasse), second class (zweite Klasse), supplement (Zuschlag). In addition, it would be advisable to learn German numbers so that you understand the fares you are being charged and times of trains: although English is widely and well spoken in West Germany, this is not necessarily the case in the East where until recently Russian was generally the first foreign language taught in schools.

The 24 hour clock is generally used for train times, but where it is not watch out for a peculiarity of the German language: halb zehn (literally half ten) does not mean half past ten but half past nine (half way to ten rather than half an hour past nine).

Note too that when reading German, the letter ß = ss (eg Straße, Strasse = street).

Opening Hours

Shops are generally open Monday to Friday from 0900-1800, except in Berlin where hours tend to be 1000-1900. On Saturdays, large stores open in the morning, but nearly all shops are closed on Saturday afternoons and Sundays.

Museums and galleries have no fixed closing day, but many tend to close on Mondays.

Money

Since July 1990 all of Germany has had the same currency, the Deutsche Mark. There is no shortage of banks or exchange booths where money can be changed. Banks are generally open from 0830 or 0900 to 1500 or 1600 Monday to Friday. Eurocheques and credit cards are widely accepted.

A Word of Warning

The whole of eastern Europe is in turmoil, but eastern Germany is a special case as it represents a whole country that has disappeared and which is being assimilated into a different state. This means that it is the subject of unprecedented change. Names are still undergoing change (the old GDR city of Karl-Marx-Stadt reverted to its old name Chemnitz after unification) and many streets that were named after leading communist figures have been renamed so as to eliminate references to the GDR's socialist past. So be wary of maps which may be out of date. Similarly, hotels and restaurants are undergoing constant changes of name as old state owned enterprises are taken over by new private owners.

ITINERARIES IN EASTERN GERMANY

Any visit to eastern Germany should certainly include Berlin and Potsdam. For travellers interested in German culture and history, Dresden and Weimar should not be missed. Leipzig, eastern Germany's second largest city, has particular interest for rail enthusiasts. Other cities of interest include Erfurt in the southwest and Schwerin in the north.

If time permits, eastern Germany has several very pleasant rural areas. Of these, Thuringia (which also contains many small towns, each with specific attractions) is perhaps the most rewarding. Other areas worth exploration include the Spreewald (accessible as a day trip from Berlin), the Harz mountains and the Mecklenburg Lake District.

BERLIN

Berlin, once the symbol of the cold war and a divided Germany, is now the capital of the united Federal Republic of Germany and arguably one of the most exciting cities in Europe. Until unification, West Berlin was a western island in the middle of the GDR, cut off from the Federal Republic and the rest of western Europe by the Berlin wall. It could be reached by plane only by means of one of the air corridors and by train by crossing the border at Helmstedt after which the train travelled through the GDR without stopping until it passed through the wall into West Berlin, ultimately stopping at West Berlin's main station, Zoologischer Garten (generally referred to simply as Bahnhof Zoo). Berlin is the largest city in eastern Europe and a good place to start a rail tour of eastern Europe. National and international trains run regularly in all directions, calling at one or more of Berlin's main line stations, Zoo, Hauptbahnhof, Friedrichstraße or Lichtenberg.

No city in central or eastern Europe has been as profoundly affected as Berlin by the changes brought by the cold war and its ending, and nowhere else has this been so clearly reflected in its transport system. On August 13 1961 all transport links between the British, American and French zones (West Berlin) and the rest of East Germany were cut, and although the Berlin S-Bahn ('overground' city rapid-transit railway) continued to be run by the Deutsche Reichsbahn (East German State Railways) it was boycotted by West Berliners, especially after a strike in September 1980 by the DR's West Berlin staff in pursuit of a free trade union like Solidarity. It deteriorated until January 1984 when West Berlin took over lines in the western zones and launched a DM1bn investment programme, paying rent for use of the north-south S-Bahn tunnel through East Berlin (where trains only stopped at Friedrichstraße, the main crossing point with Checkpoint Charlie into East Berlin) and for through trains from West Germany.

The city's rail network is based on the *Stadtbahn*, the east-west main line built in 1882 from Westkreuz through Charlottenburg, Zoologischer Garten (the famous Zoo station), Friedrichstraße, Alexanderplatz, Hauptbahnhof, and Ostkreuz, and on the

Verbindungsbahn, the north-south S-Bahn tunnel built in 1936 to link the old routes from the Nordbahnhof and the Anhalter Bahnhof via Friedrichstraße. Linking with these is a complicated network of other S-Bahn and U-Bahn (underground) routes, as well as outer-suburban Regional routes. An inner ring line linked Westkreuz and Ostkreuz, both via Gesundbrunnen to the north and via Tempelhof to the south; this was built in 1877 and then severed by the wall, but S-Bahn service was restored on the southern part by the end of 1993 (as S45, from Schönefeld to Westend, and S46, from Grünan to Westend) and on the northern part by late 1994. The East Germans also completed an outer ring line (the *Berliner Aussenring* or BAR, electrified in the early 1980s), linking Schönefeld Airport, Potsdam, Falkenhagen, Hennigsdorf and Lichtenberg, and now used for Regional services (R1/R12 to the south, R4/R14 to the west, and R10/R14 to the north and east).

After reunification full services were rapidly restored along the Stadtbahn, linking the centres of West and East Berlin, and the closed stations on S1/S2 between Nordbahnhof and Anhalter Bahnhof, such as Unter den Linden, were restored and reopened from September 1990 (before formal reunification) with temporary platforms at Bornholmer Straße (to the north) allowing West Berlin's S1/S2 to connect with East Berlin's S8/S10. In November 1993 U2, which had been operated in two separate halves in East and West Berlin, was finally reopened between Mohrenstraße and Nollendorfplatz; this required the closure of the experimental M-Bahn (magnetic-levitation line) past Potsdamer Platz. The western branches of U1 and U2 were swapped around, so that U1 now runs from Krumme Lanke to Schlesisches Tor (with extension to Warschauer Straße, on the Stadtbahn, in 1995), and U2 from Ruhleben to Pankow Vinetastraße.

Most of the other work has focused on outer-suburban links, restoring the outer ends of lines severed in 1961; the first three to reopen, in 1992, were S3 from Wannsee to Potsdam Stadt in the southwest, S1 from Frohnau to Hohen Neuendorf and Oranienburg in the north, and S2 from Lichtenrade to Mahlow and Blankenfelde in the south. S2 is also being extended north from Schönholz to Tegel, and then to Hennigsdorf, as well as on a branch southwest from Priesterweg to Lichterfelde and Teltow. R9/R10 may also be extended from Albrechtshof to Spandau and Jungfernheide, to the northwest. Until electrification is restored these are to operate with diesel units, possibly converted to pick up current on the electrified lines as well. The present 244km S-Bahn network will grow by 127km by 1995; in the long term a new North-South tunnel is proposed via a new central station at Lehrter (one stop west of Friedrichstraße).

Both systems use the same power supplies, 750V dc third-rail for the S-Bahn and 15kV ac overhead for main lines, but there are differences in the signalling, so that the fleets have not been merged, although some DR (East German) Class 243 (renumbered as Cl.143) units have been transferred to Mannheim and Dortmund, with others being modified for push-pull work in Nürnberg and Düsseldorf. The West Berlin S-Bahn's 'Olympia' Cl.275 trains, dating from 1927, are being replaced from 1993 by the new Cl.480 and Cl.485. East Berlin has aged Cl.227 units and more modern Cl.270 stock from the LEW (now AEG) works at Henningsdorf.

Now that the main line from Hannover to Berlin has been electrified, Berlin is also integrated into the (West) German networks of InterCity and InterRegio trains, with IC trains from Frankfurt (Main) every two hours, taking just under five hours, almost half an hour faster than the previous service with a change to a diesel-hauled train at Hannover. Other IC trains run from Basel and Karlsruhe to Berlin, via Dortmund or Frankfurt (Main), and there are two new IC routes, IC7 from Hamburg to Dresden via Berlin and IC8 from Munich to Berlin via Leipzig. Initially the DB's fantastic new ICE (InterCity Express) trains could not use the Stadtbahn through central Berlin but had to run around the outer ring to Berlin-Schönefeld airport, Schöneweide and Lichtenberg (all developed as main-line stations by the DR in the 1980s), but with resignalling of the Stadtbahn complete they can now run via Zoo station. New shorter ICE-2 units with about 400 seats will be introduced for these routes from 1996, based at the Rummelsberg depot. Most other mainline trains are hauled by the DR's Cl.232 (formerly Cl.132) diesels and Cl.143 (formerly Cl.243) electric locomotives, the latter so successful a design that

many are now being used in western Germany in preference to
home-grown designs.

The **U-Bahn** dates from 1902, but much of the network in
West Berlin was built during the Cold War largely as a substitute
for the virtually defunct S-Bahn. It is to be extended further, in
both West and East Berlin, under the DM2bn 'U-Bahn 2000'
plan; in particular line U8 is to be extended at both its northern
and southern ends, to Wittenau (connecting with S2) and
Hermannstraße (connecting with the restored southern ring). U5
is also to be extended west from Friedrichstraße to the Reichstag.
DM450m is being spent on resignalling, and new trains capable
of automatic operation are to be ordered. Some stations in east
Berlin have changed their names: Otto-Grotewohl-Straße is
Mohrenstraße, Marx-Engels Platz is Hackescher Markt,
Frankfurter Tor is Rathaus Friedrichshain, Lenin Allee is
Landsberger Allee, Marchlewskistraße is Weberwiese, and
Dimitroffstraße is Eberswalder Straße; however Rosa-Luxemburg-
Platz survives for now. Trams also survive in East Berlin.

The historical division of East and West Berlin is still reflected
by the *Tarifgrenze* or Fares Boundary encircling the former
Western Berlin: travel is still subsidized for citizens of the former
DDR, so that the cheaper tickets bought in East Berlin are only
valid in West Berlin for *Ossis*, those resident in the east. In 1993
full fares were DM2.10 for a short trip, DM3.20 for two hours,
or DM12 for 24 hours; you can also buy a *Sammelkart* of five
two-hour tickets.

Bahnhof Zoo

Zoologischer Garten, or Bahnhof Zoo (literally Zoo Station,
because of its proximity to an internationally renowned zoo) is in
what was once West Berlin and was the western section of
Berlin's principal main line station. It is well served by the
underground (U-Bahn) and the city's overground S-Bahn service.
The main bus station is in the station forecourt, Hardenbergplatz.

Apart from its proximity to West Berlin's zoo (there is another
in the East) and aquarium (entrances in Hardenbergplatz and
Budapester Straße), it is only a five minute walk (turn right out
of the main entrance) from West Berlin's main shopping street,

Berlin Bahnhof Zoo

Information
0700-2200 M-F
0700-2000 Sa

London Victoria 19½ hrs
Amsterdam 8½ hrs
Warsaw Centralna 9 hrs

0730-2200 M-Sa
0800-1900 Su
Outside station in
Hardenberger Platz

0600-2200

0530-2230

As restaurant above but
nearby many 24hrs

Reservation
0530-2200

3 x 10pf

24hrs DM2

24hrs

0600-2200

24hrs

Ibis
Pension Kant
Kantstrasse

BERLIN
BAHNHOF ZOO

Schweizerhof

Am Zoo

Hardenberg

Intercontinental

Kurfürstendamm

the Kurfürstendamm (Ku'damm), and from West Berlin's most photographed church, the Kaiser-Wilhelm-Gedächtniskirche (in Breitscheidplatz). The original church was constructed 1891-95 but was bombed during the Second World War. The remains of the church tower have been preserved as a memorial and the church replaced by a modern building of coloured glass that is particularly dramatic when lit up after dark.

Close to the church is West Berlin's Europa Centre, often mentioned as a tourist attraction, but in fact little more than a shopping centre. Between the two is the Weltkugelbrunnen, an elaborate fountain constructed in 1983 of bronze and granite.

The majority of sights of real historic interest are not, however, in what used to be West Berlin, but in the former East. Nevertheless, there are things worth seeing. For example, Schloß Charlottenburg (nearest U-Bahn, Richard-Wagner-Platz) is worth a visit, and anyone interested in railways will want to visit the Museum für Verkehr und Technik (Trebbiner Straße 9, nearest station U-Bahnhof Gleisdreieck) with its collection of historic locomotives displayed on the site of the goods yard of one of Berlin's most famous but now defunct goods stations, Anhalter Güterbahnhof.

Tourist Information Centre

The tourist information office (where you can reserve hotel rooms) at Bahnhof Zoo is often busy and information is limited; there is one in the Europa Centre facing on to Budapester Straße which is usually worth the walk. Opening hours at the Bahnhof Zoo office are 0800-2300 Monday to Saturday. At the Europa Centre, information office opening hours are 0800-2230 Monday-Saturday and 0900-2100 on Sunday.

Accommodation near Zoo and in West Berlin

There are many places to stay in the Charlottenburg district to the west of Zoo, as well as those listed around the Zoo below.

Upper range

Bristol Hotel Kempinski, Kurfürstendamm 27, Berlin 15 (Tel 8 84 30) with double rooms from DM470 a night.

Art Hotel Sorat, Joachimstaler Straße 28-29, Berlin 15 (Tel 8 844 70) with single rooms from DM210 and double rooms from DM250.
Schweizerhof Inter-Continental, Budapester Straße 21-31, Berlin 30 (tel 26 96 0) — single rooms DM295, double rooms DM355. Hotel Inter-Continental, Budapester Straße 2 (same prices and reservation number as the Schweizerhof).

Middle range
Hotel Hardenberg, Joachimstaler Straße 39-40, Berlin 12 (tel 8 81 41 83), single rooms from DM165, double rooms from DM255. Hotel Frühling am Zoo, Kurfürstendamm 17, Berlin 15 (tel 8 81 80 83), single rooms from DM180, double rooms from DM236.

Budget
Hotel Ibis Berlin Messe, Messedamm 10, Berlin 19 (tel 30 39 30), single rooms from DM154, double rooms from DM198. This hotel is at the main coach station, a 10 minute ride by bus 149 (night bus 49) from Bahnhof Zoo.

Pension
Pension Kant, Kantstraße has 20 rooms and it is 5 minutes from Bahnhof Zoo by bus 149.

Youth hostel
Reservations are recommended two weeks before arrival, especially in summer. For central reservations, telephone 404 16 10.
Jugendherberge Ernst Reuter, Hermsdorfer Damm 48, Berlin 28 (juniors DM17.90, over 27, DM20.90).
Jugendgästehaus, Kluckstraße 3, Berlin 30 (U-Bahn line 3 to Kurfürstenstraße — this is in fact the nearest youth hostel to the Zoo) (juniors DM22, over 27, DM25).

Berlin Friedrichstrasse

Information	0530-2230		
100 5 50	0730-1930 M-F 0900-1700 Sa, Su	✕	0630-2000
1 2	0530-2230	🍷	0630-2000
Reservation	0530-2230	👩 👨	10pf x 3
🔑	24hrs (DM 2 x 1)	✉	None
🧳	None	☎	24hrs

Albrechtstrasse

⊞ H

*Hospiz am
Bahnhof*

BERLIN
FRIEDRICHSTRASSE

R. Spree

Friedrichstrasse

⊞ H
Metropol

Unter den Linden   ⊞ H *Unter den Linden*

⊞ H
Grand

Bahnhof Friedrichstraße

Friedrichstraße station is the next main line stop after Bahnhof Zoo, and before the Berlin Wall came down was the rail border crossing point between East and West Berlin, not just for main line trains, but also for the U-Bahn and S-Bahn. Nowadays it has lost its importance as a main line station, but it is still convenient because Friedrichstraße was (and is becoming again) one of the main roads of East Berlin, and the station is only a short walk from the most famous street in the old capital of the GDR, Unter den Linden, at the west end of which is the Brandenburg Gate, one of Berlin's best known landmarks. It is still a good starting point for a tour of East Berlin.

Accommodation
Upper range
Maritim Grand Hotel, Friedrichstraße 158-164, 1080 Berlin (tel 23 27 0), and with single rooms at DM395-515 and doubles at DM480-580 (suites range from DM700-3400) the Grand is definitely in the luxury bracket, although the rather extravagant round swimming pool is not actually that good for swimming.

Hotel Metropol, Friedrichstraße 150-153, 1080 Berlin (tel 23 87 5) overlooks Friedrichstraße station is the sort of monolithic structure that was a familiar feature of communist architecture, but was excellent value for Western money in the days of the GDR. Now with single room prices ranging from DM320-385 and double rooms from DM550-1200 it is again in the upper range. It has an excellent gym and swimming pool.

Middle range
Hotel Unter den Linden, Unter den Linden 14, 1080 Berlin, (tel 23 81 10), single rooms from DM185 and double rooms from DM260.

Budget
Hospiz am Bahnhof Friedrichstraße Albrechtstraße 8, Berlin (tel 282 5321). Single from DM48, twin from DM77. Comfortable, central and very good value. It is run by church groups and prices vary according to facilities in the room (ie colour TV, showers etc). Reservations advisable (160 beds).

Hostels and camping
See Lichtenberg.

Alexanderplatz

Alexanderplatz (Alexander Square) is only two stops on the S-Bahn from Friedrichstraße (the S-Bahn line runs along the same route as the main line trains between Zoo, Friedrichstraße and Alexanderplatz, and from there on to East Berlin's two other main line stations, Hauptbahnhof and Lichtenberg), but most sights worth seeing in what was the centre of the former GDR capital can best be seen on foot and are found between Friedrichstraße and Alexanderplatz.

Walking along Unter den Linden away from the Brandenburg Gate and towards Alexanderplatz you pass the Staatsbibliothek (State Library), the Humboldt University, the Neue Wache (New Watch or Guard House) and the Zeughaus (Arsenal), formerly a museum of communist history, all on the left, and the Alte Bibliothek (Old Library) and the State Opera House on your right. In the middle of Unter den Linden on the central promenade stands Rauch's statue of Frederick the Great. Crossing over the river Spree, ahead of you on the left is the restored Berlin cathedral, now really a museum and concert hall. (The catholic cathedral of St Hedwig, a distinctive, round church building, is just behind the opera house.) Opposite the cathedral is a huge modern building with reflecting glass, a common feature of modern architecture of the GDR. This is the Palace of the Republic (Palast der Republik). It used to house the GDR parliament (Volkskammer) as well as cafés and cinemas, but was closed after unification. Rumour has it that it is to be demolished and perhaps even replaced by a replica of the Berliner Schloß, the huge palace that once stood here but which was destroyed in the Second World War. Nearby, stand two enormous statues of Marx and Engels, rare survivors of East Berlin's communist past.

The Red Town Hall (Rotes Rathaus) which can be seen from here gets its name from the colour of its brickwork and not from the GDR's communist past. Nearby is the Nikolaiviertel, an area of restored shops, houses, cafés and restaurants takes its name from the church of St Nicholas, now a museum.

Just to the west of Alexanderplatz, and looking rather out of place in the shadow of the TV tower, is the Marienkirche (St Mary's Church), one of the first monuments in East Berlin to be restored after the war. The TV tower itself is open for visitors (the viewing platform is 207 metres high).

Passing under the railway line and past Alexanderplatz station you enter Alexanderplatz itself, once regarded as the proud centre of the GDR's capital city, but now rather desolate, as many of the shops are closed, and buildings on the square are undergoing restoration.

No visit to the eastern part of Berlin is complete without a visit to the Museuminsel (the 'museum island' between the Humboldt University and the cathedral). This little island in the Spree is the location of the Pergamonmuseum (ancient art and sculpture), the Bodemuseum (again concentrating on the ancient world, but also containing collections of coins, sculptures and paintings), the Nationalgalerie (modern painting) and the Altes Museum (engravings and modern art). Because Berlin was divided, West Berlin still has its own museum and art gallery in Dahlem (U-Bahn station Dahlem Dorf is the best way to get there). Some reorganisation of Berlin's museums and collections is currently taking place to overcome this unnatural divide.

Also worth seeing are the restored Französischer Dom and Deutscher Dom, two huge symmetrical cathedrals which dominate the Gendarmenmarkt, not far from Friedrichstraße. The Gendarmenmarkt is also the site of the Schauspielhaus, East Berlin's main concert hall.

Alexanderplatz Tourist Information Centre
Located under the TV tower; the staff are friendly and efficient.

Reisburo, located at Alexanderplatz 5, is more than a travel agency with services including car hire and excursions. From here you can obtain a *Berlin Falkplan* (see Getting around in Berlin), or you can consult any of the travel businesses on the premises.

Accommodation
The Forum Hotel, Alexanderplatz, 1020 Berlin (tel 23 89 0), formerly the Stadt Berlin, single rooms DM195-275, double

Berlin Hauptbahnhof

 0515-2230

London Victoria 20 hrs
Warsaw Centralna 8½ hrs
Amsterdam 9 hrs, Oslo 21 hrs

0700-1930 M-F
0700-1800 Sa
0800-1600 Su

 0630-2230

 24hrs

 0630-2230

 0600-2000

24hrs, 3 x 10pf
In basement
Also showers

 24hrs DM2

 None

 0600-2300

 24hrs

Locations of airports and principal stations

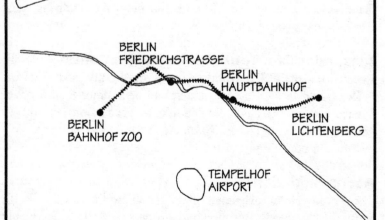

rooms DM245-325), was the first modern hotel built in the centre of East Berlin.

Hauptbahnhof

The largest railway station in what was once East Berlin, the capital of the GDR, was originally called the Schlesischer Bahnhof (Silesian station). It was then renamed Berlin Ostbahnhof (Eastern station) and renamed again as the Berlin Hauptbahnhof (which, rather prosaically, just means Berlin main station) in December 1987. It has recently undergone substantial renovation: the three storey interior provides a wide range of facilities, and a series of archways in tilework covers the formerly rather shabby exterior. Trains leave from the Hauptbahnhof for Dresden, Frankfurt an der Oder, Gera, Halle, Jena, Leipzig, Stralsund and other destinations in the five new Federal states. Trains also leave for numerous destinations in western Germany, but generally these can also be caught from Zoo.

Just in front of the station, diagonally to the left as you come out of the main entrance, there is a section of the Berlin wall still in place, painted with murals. Otherwise the area around the Hauptbahnhof is undistinguished.

Lichtenberg

Four stops on from the Hauptbahnhof on the S-Bahn, in the direction of Ahrensfelde, is the last of East Berlin's main line stations, Lichtenberg. Trains leave from here for Halle, Leipzig, Dresden, Chemnitz, Rostock and elsewhere. Generally, it is a good station for many major domestic and international rail destinations. Like the Hauptbahnhof, Lichtenberg is designed for transit; there are few external facilities, but good S-Bahn and U-Bahn connections to the city centre and elsewhere.

Accommodation
Middle range
Hotel Nova, Weitlingstraße 15, 1130 Berlin (tel 5 25 24 66) which is in fact a modernised police station. Single rooms from DM110, double rooms from DM135, inclusive of breakfast (33 rooms). Just opposite the station.

Berlin Lichtenberg

ℹ️ Information	0530-2230		Berlin Lichtenberg 4 hrs Leipzig 1½ hrs Eisenach 1 hr
💵	None in station, but Deutsche Bank opposite main entrance in Weitlingstrasse	🍴	0700-2200
📰	0530-2230	🍷	0700-2200
Ⓑ Reservation	0530-2230	🚺 🚹	24hrs Also showers
🔑	24hrs DM2 x 1	✉️	None
🧳	24hrs	☎️	24hrs

Youth Hostel

Jugendhotel am Tierpark, Franz Mett Straße 7, 1136 Berlin (tel 51 00 114) with single rooms from DM45 and twin rooms from DM60 a night. Close to Lichtenberg (two stops away on U-Bahn line 5 and close to Tierpark station).

Getting around in Berlin

To get the most out of Berlin you will find the **Berlin Falkplan** (which includes Potsdam) useful; it is a clever A-Z map of the city that is pocket sized but need not be unfolded all at once. It contains an index of street names, details of transport routes, and costs about DM9. The Schnellbahnnetz plan, produced by Berlin's transport authority (the BVG), is available free from U-Bahn stations and BVG information centres. It also forms the

centrefold of the free magazine BVG Aktuell, again available free
of charge. It is a colour coded map of all stations in and around
Berlin.

Berlin has an efficient public transport system consisting not
just of the U-Bahn and S-Bahn, but of a vast network of bus
routes, and in the eastern part of the city there is still a well
developed tram network. Fares are relatively cheap. A single
ticket costs DM3.50, but covers one whole journey provided it is
completed within two hours, permitting unlimited changes and
interruptions to your journey. Journeys of up to three stops by S-
Bahn or U-Bahn or up to six bus stops are charged at DM2.30
(Kurzstreckentarif). Instead of buying individual tickets, you can
buy a card (Sammelkarte) for DM12 which enables you to make
four journeys. For DM13 you can buy a Berlin-Ticket that gives
you unlimited travel for 24 hours. A six day ticket costs DM33,
or, if you are staying for a month, the so-called Umweltkarte will
cost you DM82. Special family cards are also available.

There are few ticket offices (at many stations you can only
purchase tickets from machines) and no ticket collectors, but there
are inspectors who will check whether your ticket is valid. Before
you travel you must insert your ticket into one of the ticket
machines (Entwerter) which stamps the ticket with the date and
time you start your journey.

Food and Drink

There is a huge variety of restaurants and cuisine available in
Berlin, from traditional German to the ubiquitous hamburger and
pizza.

The Kneipe (a traditional pub/restaurant) offers traditional
German food, generally inexpensively. The Gaststätte is much the
same but tends to be more expensive and elaborate. The Pub or
Bierstube sells beer. You do not normally buy rounds, but the
waiter or waitress will mark your beer mat or keep a record of
what you order, and you pay at the end.

For quick snacks you may wish to try a Stehcafé, but do not
expect to rest — in a Stehcafé you eat standing at high tables;
there are no seats.

Berlin is famous for its opulent cafés, which serve full meals but are best known for their coffee and cakes (Kaffee und Kuchen). They serve a whole range of coffee types and a vast variety of cakes and pastries. Try the Kranzler at the corner of Kurfürstendamm and Joachimstaler Straße or further up the Ku'damm the Mohring at the corner of Uhlandstraße. The Café Einstein (Kurfürstenstraße 58 — the nearest U-Bahn is Nollendorfplatz) is especially recommended.

In the East, as you might expect, many cafés and restaurants have changed hands. The hotels offer good food but tend to be expensive. Better value are the restaurants and cafés in the Nikolaiviertel. Especially popular (on the edge of the Nikolaiviertel) is Mutter Hoppe not far from the Red Town Hall.

The town hall, in common with many in Germany, has a restaurant in the cellar (Ratskeller). Ratskeller generally serve traditional German food at mid-range prices.

Excursions

If your time in Berlin is limited, take the 100 bus as it links the East and the West of the city and passes many of Berlin's best known landmarks. It runs during the day and at night. (With a two hour ticket, you are free to get on and off.) It leaves from Bahnhof Zoo and goes to Alexanderplatz.

On the outskirts of Berlin there are numerous lakes and woods. The Wannsee can be reached on the S-Bahn, as can the Nikolassee and the Grunewald and Grunewaldsee (See means lake as well as sea in German, although the gender of the two words is different). Perhaps the most famous lake in the East is the Müggelsee, Berlin's largest lake (the nearest stations are Friedrichshagen or Rahnsdorf on the S-Bahn).

Potsdam

Any visitor to Berlin should try to visit Potsdam too. There are plenty of bus excursions from the centre of Berlin, but trains leave from Hauptbahnhof and pass through Friedrichstraße and Zoo. From Zoo the journey takes about 20 minutes. The town centre has been well restored. Try to visit the splendid Nikolaikirche (St Nicholas church) and the old garrison church (Garnisonkirche): Potsdam has always been a military town. Also worth visiting are the Dutch Quarter (Holländisches Viertel), the area of the town settled by the Dutch in the 18th Century, and the Russian Colony (Russische Kolonie), founded originally for the benefit of twelve Russian singers (Prussian prisoners of war) by Friedrich Wilhelm III in 1826.

Undoubtedly the main attraction of Potsdam is the Park Sanssouci. The extensive park is the location of the Sanssouci Palace, and a whole range of other architectural attractions — a Chinese teahouse, orangery, mausoleum, Neptune grotto, Sicilian garden, New Palace (Neues Palais) and even Roman baths (Römische Bäder), the majority built in the 18th Century.

Also of interest is the Cecilienhof Palace. Built during 1913 in mock English Tudor style, it functions partly as a museum commemorating the Potsdam conference that decided the fate of Germany (and of much of Europe) after the Second World War but is also a hotel.

Spreewald

Also close to Berlin is the Spreewald, an area of streams and canals, tributaries and offshoots of the river Spree, set in attractive woodland. Trains leave for Lübbenau or Cottbus from Berlin-Lichtenberg or Berlin-Schöneweide, although there are plenty of coach excursions as well.

The Spreewald is the homeland of the Sorbs, a Slav people who have their own language (referred to as Sorbian, Wendish or Lusatian), which is distantly related to Polish, and their own distinctive culture (which enjoyed protection under the constitution of the GDR).

The town of Lübbenau contains the Spreewaldmuseum, which is devoted to Sorb culture and the traditions of the region. Cottbus and Lübbenau are both good places from which to enjoy a boat trip along the narrow channels in the large, punt-like boats that are traditional in this area. Motor boats are not permitted, and many residents still use traditional river transport to carry farm animals or hay.

Dresden Hauptbahnhof

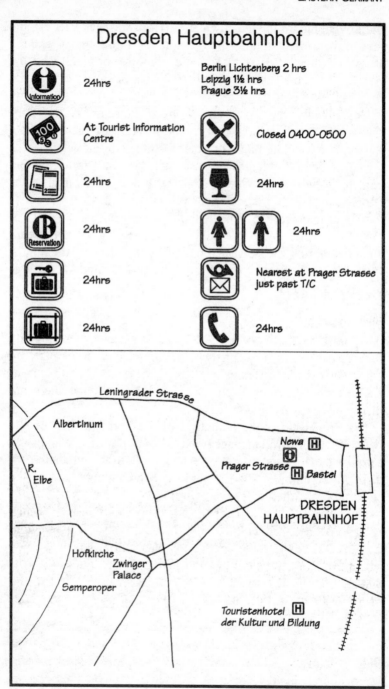

24hrs

At Tourist Information Centre

24hrs

24hrs

24hrs

24hrs

Berlin Lichtenberg 2 hrs
Leipzig 1½ hrs
Prague 3½ hrs

Closed 0400-0500

24hrs

24hrs

Nearest at Prager Strasse
just past T/C

24hrs

Leningrader Strasse

Albertinum

R. Elbe

Newa

Prager Strasse
Bastei

DRESDEN HAUPTBAHNHOF

Hofkirche
Zwinger
Palace
Semperoper

Touristenhotel
der Kultur und Bildung

DRESDEN

Dresden is the ancient capital of the rulers of Saxony and now the administrative centre of Sachsen (Saxony) in the south east of eastern Germany. It lies on the banks of the river Elbe, and barge transport links it to the North Sea and Bremen. Heading south, freight barges travel to the Danube and the Black Sea. The city is close to the border with the Czech Republic, with which the Erzgebirge (Erz mountains) form a natural boundary.

At first sight on leaving the railway station, you may wonder why you stopped. Tall, featureless blocks of flats and hotels disguise the architectural heritage nearer the Elbe. Dresden was largely destroyed in air raids in February 1945, and, although reconstruction of the historic centre began soon after the war, parts of the town are marred by ugly modern building and, even now, by the remains of war damage.

Pragerstraße is the main pedestrian thoroughfare from the Hauptbahnhof (main station) towards the old city. Look out for the modern fountains in front of the tourist information office and continue straight ahead, passing Altmarkt (old market) and the Kreuzkirche (Church of the Cross), taking its name from a splinter of the cross on which Christ died, allegedly held in the church, until you enter the domain of the kings of Saxony.

Although still in ruins, the Schloß (Royal Palace) retains a quiet dignity. Nearby, the Zwinger (literally translated, 'keep'), built in the early 18th Century and consisting of several pavilions connected by a one-storey gallery, is often considered one of Germany's finest baroque buildings. Here and in the nearby Albertinum Dresden's famous collection of old masters is housed (during reconstruction work, the exact locations vary). The Albertinum also houses many other treasures, including 19th and 20th Century paintings, the Green Vault (a collection of gold, silver and jewellery), coins and sculptures. Next to the Albertinum is the Brühlsche Terrasse (Brühl Terrace), terraced gardens with wonderful views of the Elbe.

Close to the Zwinger is the Semperoper (Semper opera house), constructed during 1838-41, destroyed in 1945 and reopened in 1985. Next to the Schloß is the Hofkirche (Court Cathedral), the largest church in Saxony, with the bodies of 49 of the Saxon kings and princes in its vaults.

Other sites of note in Dresden include the ruins of the Frauenkirche, left as a memorial to those who died in the bombing, the Langer Gang (Long Passage) behind the Hofkirche, and the Japanese Palace, just north of the river Elbe.

Railway enthusiasts may also be interested in the Verkehrsmuseum (Transport Museum) in the Johanneum, west of the Neumarkt. The collection includes the Muldenthal, a steam locomotive built in Chemnitz in 1861 and the oldest original steam locomotive remaining in East Germany.

Tourist Information
Pragerstraße 10-11 (tel 4 40 31), about five minutes from the Hauptbahnhof. It is open 0900-2000 Monday to Saturday and 0900-1400 on Sunday.

Accommodation
Upper range
Hotel Newa, Leningraderstraße (tel 96 71 12); single from DM179; twin from DM197.
Bellevue, Köpckestraße, on the banks of the Elbe (tel 5 66 20); single from DM200 and double from DM320.

Medium range
Hotel Bastei (tel 4 85 60); single from DM72 and double from DM99, on the Pragerstraße just opposite the Hotel Newa.

Budget
Contact the tourist information office for details of pensions and private rooms (between DM20 and DM80).

Youth hostel
Jugendherberge Rudi Arndt, Huberstraße 11, O-8027 Dresden (tel 47 06 67); juniors DM14.50 and seniors DM17.50.

Camping
Mockritz, Boderitznerstraße 8, O-8020 Dresden (tel 47 82 26).

Excursions

From Dresden it is well worth considering a few excursions. Try and allow a full day for both Swiss Saxony and Meißen and a half day for Pillnitz.

Swiss Saxony

A boat from near Brühlsche Terrasse will take you on the River Elbe towards Swiss Saxony. The scenery is spectacular as you approach the gorge where the river cuts through the mountains. You will also see terraces of vines and woodlands.

Meißen

Among East Germany's many attractive small towns, Meißen is unique in offering a picturesque setting on the banks of the river Elbe, a historic town centre, virtually unscathed by the Second World War, and a variety of specialities from its world famous porcelain to local wine. The porcelain factory is about 1.5km south of the town centre (close to Meißen-Triebischtal station), and the museum and show workshop are open every day except Monday. In the town itself, the group of buildings on the Castle Hill (the Cathedral, Albrechts Castle and the former Bishops Castle) are well worth a visit.

The tourist information office (An der Frauenkirche, tel 44 70) arranges tours of the town and surrounding area and can also arrange private accommodation.

Schloß Pillnitz

Pillnitz is a small complex of palaces set in beautiful grounds on the banks of the Elbe. It can be reached by boat or by the number 85 bus from the centre of Dresden. The palaces were the summer residences of the kings of Saxony and contain some of the world's most impressive examples of 18th Century chinoiserie.

ERFURT

Although little known outside Germany, Erfurt is an attractive city as well as the administrative centre and capital of Thuringia. In 1992, the city of Erfurt celebrated its 1250th anniversary, and

Erfurt Hauptbahnhof

 24hrs

Berlin Lichtenberg 4 hrs
Leipzig 1½ hrs
Eisenach 1 hr

 0830-1945 T-F
1000-1600 Sa-Su

 0530-2200 (on platform 1)

 0600-2200

 0530-2200 (on platform 1)

 0600-2100

 24hrs
(on platform 1)

 24hrs

 None

0630-1730 M-F
0730-1430 Sa-Su

 24hrs (Outside on
Willy-Brandt-Platz)

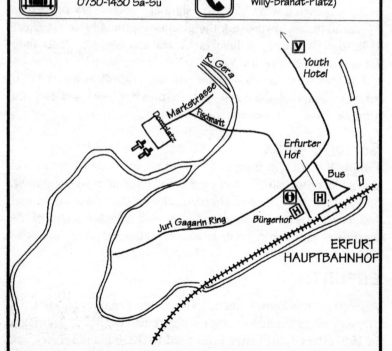

a walk around the old town reveals a wide range of historical monuments.

Visitors to Erfurt can scarcely fail to be impressed by the twin sights of the Gothic cathedral (Dom) and the 14th Century Church of St Severus (Severikirche) standing side by side at the top of a flight of 70 steps on a rocky outcrop looking down on the town. In addition to its religious significance, the town grew to prominence because of its position at the centre of an early trade route between east and west. Medieval timbered buildings which belonged to merchants and shop keepers are still to be found in the centre of the old town.

Easily manageable walks from the Fischmarkt (Fish Market) down the Marktstraße to the Domplatz (Cathedral Square) or from the Anger (meaning village green, but now a pedestrianised area), across the Krämerbrücke (Krämer Bridge) to the Augustinian Monastery (Augustinerkloster) where Martin Luther studied, would include many of the most picturesque and historically interesting sights.

The Krämer Bridge (Krämer means shopkeeper) across the river Gera, little more than a stream today, is lined by 32 small shops mostly selling antiques and works of art and is the only bridge north of the Alps to be lined on both sides by timbered houses.

Erfurt is a good place to stay. Although it is quieter than many German cities, it has a good selection of restaurants and hotels. Rail links are also good, especially to other parts of Thuringia.

Tourist Information

Tourist information is at Bahnhofstraße 37, 99084 Erfurt (tel 5 62 33 55); open Monday to Friday 1000-1800; on Saturdays and Sundays it is at Krämerbrücke 3. The tourist information office can help arrange accommodation in private rooms. It also publishes a free monthly magazine (*Erfurt Magazin*) with details of events in and around Erfurt.

Accommodation
Upper range
Erfurter Hof, Willy-Brandt-Platz 1 (just in front of the station; tel

53 10); single from DM150 and double from DM200.
Bauer Hotel Excelsior, Bahnhofstraße 35, 99084 Erfurt (also
close to the station; tel 5 67 00); single from DM149 and double
from DM189.

Medium range
Hotel am Ring, Juri-Gagarin-Ring 148 (tel 6 46 55 20); single
from DM65 and double from DM95.

Budget
Hotel Bürgerhof, near Tourist Information, from DM40.
Private rooms (contact Tourist Information)

Youth hostel
Hochheimer Straße 12, 99094 Erfurt (tel 5 62 67 05), 5km from
the centre (take tram number 5 from the Hauptbahnhof to the
terminus; it is then a 2 minute walk away). There are no camping
sites nearby.

Restaurants
There is a fairly wide choice of restaurants in Erfurt; for medium
and high priced meals, try the area near the Rathaus (Haus zur
güldenen Sonne, Michaelisstraße 37; Zum Augustiner, Michaelisstraße 32 etc). For cheaper meals and fast food, the area near the
station should be explored. Railway fans might like to visit the
Dampflok (steam train) Pub in the Erfurterhof, which has railway
decorations and serves Erfurt beer, as well as draught Guinness.

THURINGIA

South and west of Erfurt lies the Thuringian Forest (Thüringer
Wald). This area, with its small traditional towns, woods, hills
and rivers, is one of the most picturesque parts of the former
GDR, and an ideal place for walking holidays, as well as for
other outdoor and cultural activities. Allow at least one week to
experience this beautiful area. Towns of particular interest include
Eisenach, Gotha, Suhl, Meiningen and Schmalkalden, but there
are many other places worth short visits (Arnstadt, where J.S.

Bach was organist, Ilmenau, with many Goethe associations, and Saalfeld with its 'fairy grottos').

Eisenach

Eisenach is well-known for two reasons: it is here that Martin Luther worked on his translation of the New Testament from Greek into German; it is also the birthplace of J.S. Bach. To reach Eisenach, take the train from Erfurt (about one hour's journey), or travel on from Gotha (about 45 minutes).

The Wartburg Castle which stands above Eisenach is a pleasant 45 minutes' walk through woods from the station (you can ride the last part by donkey); alternatively you can take a bus from opposite the station. The castle was founded in 1067 and is one of the most beautiful in Germany. A tour of the interior includes the enormous banqueting hall on the second floor, an excellent collection of works of art including paintings by Lucas Cranach, and the Lutherstube (Luther's room) which contains the Bible and other articles which he used during his stay at the Wartburg. The castle opens daily 0830-1600 and an early visit is recommended.

As travellers Leon and Phoebe Spence point out, 'The walk through the nature reserve to the Wartburg is a pleasant preparation to appreciate the castle. Unfortunately, there were coach loads to detract from the air of authenticity and the queues put us off a tour of the interior. Perhaps we should have given the donkeys some business to experience authenticity.

J.S. Bach was born at Eisenach in 1685 and the Bachhaus at Am Frauenplan 21 contains a collection of articles relating to the life and works of the whole Bach family. There is also a bronze statue of Bach in the market place, close to the Pfarrkirche St Georg (parish church of St George) where Bach was baptised and where Bach's works are frequently performed.

The Wartburg car, which — with the more infamous Trabant — was one of the only two cars manufactured in the GDR, was made in Eisenach. Production of Wartburgs stopped soon after unification and the site is now used to manufacture Opel models. On the Wartburgallee there is a small display of vintage and more modern cars. This includes the EMW *Eisenachmotorwerk* which was the predecessor of today's BMW.

Gotha

Lying midway between Erfurt and Eisenach, Gotha is a lively town with an attractively restored centre. It is also from here that the Waldbahn (forest tram) starts on its route to villages in the heart of the Thuringian Forest, terminating at Tabarz or Waltershausen. Many of the villages along the line, including for example Friedrichroda, are very pleasant holiday centres with cafés, hotels and well-signposted walks through the woods.

In Gotha itself, the Schloß Friedenstein (Friedenstein palace) is worth a visit, and the free-standing Renaissance town hall and surrounding streets are an attractive area for exploration.

Suhl

Suhl can be reached by train in about an hour from Erfurt. On the final stages, the train passes through a long tunnel and makes a slow descent to Suhl.

The town is centrally placed for walking and from here, the highest mountain in the Thüringer Wald — the Großer Beerberg (987m) — is easy to reach. The town itself is quiet: evening entertainment is limited to just a few bars and a theatre.

The tourist information office is at Steinweg 1, opposite the Rotes Rathaus (red town hall). Private rooms from about DM20 per person are available (the tourist office can help with this). If you prefer a luxury hotel, try the Thüringen Suhl at Platz der Deutschen Einheit 2, which is very central. The Hotel Stadt Suhl at Puschkinstraße is also quite good, and closer to the station. Camping is at Oberhof, up in the mountains, about 30 minutes away by train or bus.

Meiningen

Just 13 minutes from Suhl and with direct rail links from Berlin (a little over five hours), lies Meiningen, one of the best places for a short stay in Thuringia. Travellers to and from the old Federal Republic should note that there is now also a rail link with Würzburg, via Schweinfurt. The town is situation in the beautiful valley of the river Werra which joins the Weser and eventually enters the North Sea at Bremen.

Schloß Elisabethenburg, formerly the ducal palace, dates

largely from 1682-92 and houses a number of museums, as well as an excellent, modestly priced, restaurant. Also of interest is the Goethe-Park, once known as the English Garden.

Meiningen has a large theatre, which was particularly famous at the beginning of the century; it is also possible to ski near here in winter.

The tourist information office is just outside the railway station. From April to October it is open 0900-1700. Upper range accommodation is available at the Hotel Schloß Landsberg but there are also many private rooms on offer at DM15 to 20 per person. As yet, there is no camping site.

Schmalkalden

This small town, about 20km north of Meiningen, is one of the oldest and most beautiful in the region. The castle, Schloß Wilhelmsburg, is now a museum. From here you have wonderful views of the valley and the mountains beyond. Apart from the castle, there are many good walks. You can see a number of spring-fed freshwater lakes and in some you can join locals for a swim.

The tourist information office is at Mohrengasse 2; it is open Monday to Friday 1000-1300 and 1400-1700 and Saturdays 1100-1400. Ask for their accommodation list or phone 003 7670 3182. Private rooms start from DM10 plus DM5 for breakfast. Several good restaurants are located on the path up to the castle.

Weimar

Still in Thuringia, and a 15 minute train journey from Erfurt, Weimar provides more attractions for those interested in German history and culture than anywhere else in East Germany with the exception of Berlin and Dresden. It can be visited as a day excursion from Erfurt and is also included in some bus tours from Berlin; there is also a variety of accommodation in Weimar itself.

Despite its fame, Weimar is a sleepy little town. Weimar has undergone two great periods of expansion. The first was in the 16th Century when extensive building work attracted people to settle here, including the painter Lucas Cranach, whose house on the Markt can still be visited. The second was in the 18th

Weimar Bahnhof

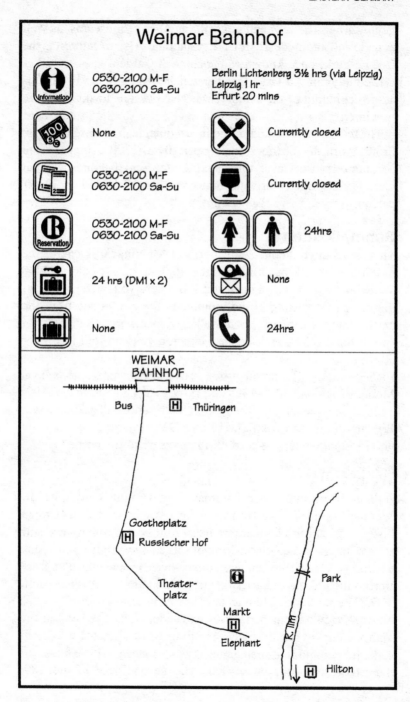

0530-2100 M-F
0630-2100 Sa-Su

Berlin Lichtenberg 3½ hrs (via Leipzig)
Leipzig 1 hr
Erfurt 20 mins

None

Currently closed

0530-2100 M-F
0630-2100 Sa-Su

Currently closed

0530-2100 M-F
0630-2100 Sa-Su

24hrs

24 hrs (DM1 x 2)

None

None

24hrs

WEIMAR
BAHNHOF

Bus   H   Thüringen

Goetheplatz
H   Russischer Hof

Theater-
platz

Markt
H

Elephant

Park

R. Ilm

H   Hilton

Century, when Bach and later some of Germany's major literary figures, including Goethe, Schiller and Herder, lived in Weimar. Goethe's house in the Frauenplan is now a museum, as is Schiller's house in the Schillerstraße. Herder's statue stands outside the Herderkirche (Herder church), also in the town centre.

Other places of interest include the Residenzschloß (the Grand Ducal Palace) which houses Weimar's impressive art collection, the Liszt museum, the Theaterplatz (Theatre Square) and the German National Theatre, an earlier version of which was the seat of the German National Assembly where the constitution of the Weimar Republic was adopted in 1919.

The parks and gardens around the town, particularly the park which runs alongside the river Ilm and includes Goethe's Garden house, give Weimar a feeling of peace and tranquillity, and make it a pleasant place for leisurely exploration.

Nearby, using the bus, are several sights of interest: the Schloß Belvedere, the former royal summer palace, to the south of the town, and Buchenwald, a former Nazi concentration camp. The site is now a national memorial to more than 56,000 Jews, communists, homosexuals and others killed between 1937 and 1945. Near the site, a large memorial built in the GDR period, dominates the hillside.

Tourist Information
Marktstraße 4, 99423 Weimar (tel 036 43 20 21 73) and is open Mondays to Fridays 0900-1900, Saturdays 0900-1600 and Sundays 1000-1600 between March and October (Mondays to Fridays 0900-1800 and Saturdays 0900-1300 November to February).

The information office can help arrange private rooms and other accommodation. It also publishes the monthly guide *Live Weimar* (DM1) with details of current events, as well as a full list of accommodation and restaurants.

Accommodation
Upper range
Weimar Hilton, Belvederer Allee 25, 99425 Weimar (tel 43 72 20). Hotel Elephant, Am Markt 19 (tel 436 14 71).

Middle range
Russischer Hof, Goetheplatz 2, 99423 Weimar (tel 77 40).

Budget
Hotel Thüringen, Brennerstraße 42, 99423 Weimar (tel 36 75); singles from DM105 and double rooms from DM160.

Restaurants
Gastmahl des Meeres, Herderplatz 16, specialises in fish dishes, the historic Weißer Schwann, Am Frauenplan, and the Ratskeller in the Markt, serves regional and international dishes.

LEIPZIG

The prime reason for a visit here by rail enthusiasts is one of Europe's largest stations, the Hauptbahnhof. Twenty-six platforms stretch behind what appear to be two stations joined together. Opened in 1915, the station is under a preservation order, and everything, from the two (east and west) halls to the 300m wide façade, is built on a monumental scale. As well as being the main line station, with connections to destinations throughout central Europe, the station also incorporates two S-Bahn lines.

Leipzig was the second city of the German Democratic Republic and today retains its industrial importance as the capital of Saxony. The historic centre has been largely restored, is mostly pedestrianised and is close to the station.

Given that the city is within a day's travelling distance of Erfurt, Dresden or even Berlin, it may not warrant an overnight stay, but if you are planning to see other parts of the south, Leipzig is a convenient staging post.

The main sites of interest in the old town are the Altes Rathaus (old town hall) with its museum of local history, containing a Mendelssohn room (the composer was conductor of the Leipzig Gewandhaus orchestra from 1835 to 1847); the Mädler Passage and Auerbach's Keller (Auerbach's cellar), where Goethe set a scene of his play Faust; the Thomaskirche (Church of St Thomas) where J.S. Bach worked as organist and choirmaster of the Thomas School between 1723 and 1750; the Augustusplatz,

Leipzig Hauptbahnhof

 0600-2200

Berlin Lichtenberg 2½ hrs
Erfurt 1½ hrs
Dresden 1½ hrs

 0700-1930 Mon-Fri
0800-1600 Sat

 Various possibilities
0500-2300

 0545-2145

 Various possibilities
0500-2300

 0545-2145

 24hrs (DM1)

 24hrs DM 2

 In 'Presse und Buch' shop
(Osthalle)
0500-2200 Mon-Sat
0600-2100 Sun

 0600-2115

 24hrs

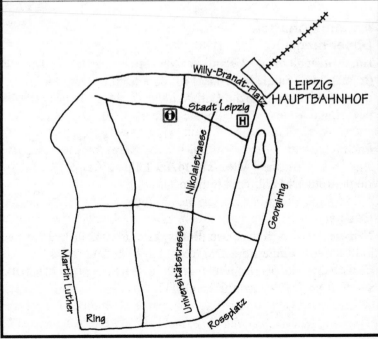

dominated by the 34-storey university building and also containing the Neues Gewandhaus (New Drapers' Hall), home of the world famous Leipzig Gewandhaus orchestra; and the Nikolaikirche, one of Leipzig's most interesting churches architecturally as well as being the church from which demonstrating crowds left for Monday evening rallies in the autumn of 1989 immediately prior to the downfall of the GDR.

After all this, you may wish to sample the café scene: in the old town you will be spoilt for choice. You may like to try the Kaffeebaum (Coffee Tree) at Kleine Fleischergasse 4, one of Europe's oldest cafés and a favourite haunt of 19th Century musicians and writers, including Goethe, Wagner and Schumann.

Tourist Information
Sachsenplatz 1, 04109 Leipzig (tel 7 95 90), open 0900-1900 Monday to Friday, 0930-1400 Saturday and Sunday. The information office can help with private accommodation. For information about events in Leipzig, buy a copy of the monthly *Leipzig Life*.

Accommodation
Upper range
Hotel Stadt Leipzig, Richard-Wagner-Straße 52, 04179 Leipzig (tel 2 14 50), single from DM180; double from DM280.
Inter-Continental Leipzig, Gerberstraße 15, 04105 Leipzig (tel 79 90); single from DM290; double from DM320.

Middle range
Am Park, Grunauer Allee 37, 04209 Leipzig (tel 4 12 61 56); single from DM122; double from DM154.

Budget
Herberge in der Buttergasse, Buttergasse 36, 04249 Leipzig (tel 3 40 08 96); single from DM70;double from DM115.
Christliches Hospiz, Roßstraße 14, 0-7010 Leipzig (tel 281 210), single from DM48, twin from DM77.

Youth hostels
Käthe-Kollwitz-Straße 64, 04109 Leipzig (tel 47 05 30); junior
DM17.50; senior DM21.00.
Am Auensee, Gustav-Esche-Straße 4, 04159 Leipzig (tel 5 71
89); junior DM14.00, senior DM17.00.

Camping
Am Auensee (address as for youth hostel; tel 2 12 30 31). To get
there, take tram 10 or 28 from the main station and then walk
south to Auensee; alternatively you can take the S-Bahn four
stops to Gustav-Esche-Straße and walk north.

Excursions
British tourists may be interested in a trip to Colditz, about 22km
southeast of Leipzig. It cannot be reached by rail, so it is
advisable to book on a group tour from Leipzig. The infamous
castle, described by Reichsmarschall Goering as escape-proof,
proved not to be so for 30 Second World War prisoners who
managed to regain their homelands. These included Airey Neave,
who later became a Conservative MP and was killed by the IRA
in 1979. Little of the interior of the castle is open to the public,
but it is worth a visit.

THE HARZ MOUNTAINS
Along with the Thüringer Wald, the Harz mountains contain
some of eastern Germany's most picturesque scenery. The area
is a favourite holiday destination, and in addition to heavily
forested peaks, fast-flowing streams, valleys, villages and
abundant wild life, it also has a magnificent, functioning steam
railway. The Harz mountains can be reached easily by rail from
Erfurt or from Berlin via Halle.
   The Harz-Querbahn, a narrow-gauge steam railway, runs from
Nordhausen in the south to various destinations further north,
including Wernigerode and Quedlinburg, a trip of around 61km.
The railway has been in use since 1899 and in summer there are
special tours along the line. The route passes through some of the
most beautiful scenery in the area and stops at several spas and

resorts.

At Nordhausen the steam railway leaves from a special station close to the mainline station. At the north of the line, both Wernigerode and Quedlinburg are worth a visit. Quedlinburg has a centre which has remained virtually intact since the middle ages. Wernigerode too has several streets lined with timber-framed houses and an attractive town hall dating from 1543.

The Harz has a wide choice of accommodation, including the Quedlinburger Hof, close to Quedlinburg station, the Handelshof, opposite Nordhausen station, and the attractively refurbished Kurhotel, at Mauerstraße 9 in Blankenburg.

MECKLENBURG-VORPOMMERN

Schwerin is a good central base for the rail traveller to explore this area. Access is good from both Berlin (two and a half hours) and Hamburg. Allow a day or two for settling in, exploring the city or neighbouring villages and lakes, and then head for Rostock. In little over an hour you can be soaking up the atmosphere of this large port. Apart from the sights of the town itself, it is possible to reach Copenhagen in five and a half hours. Denmark is just over two hours away by ferry and an easy day trip.

From Rostock, Stralsund and the island of Rügen are just a short ride away. Stralsund can be used as a base for visiting the island, but there are many other centres. Binz, one of the most popular seaside resorts on Rügen, is linked by rail and has a good range of accommodation, although this tends to be booked in summer. Saßnitz is the port for travelling to Sweden but it is too far to cross the Baltic for a day visit. Stralsund is on the main line to Berlin Lichtenberg and a comfortable three hours by rail with regular services.

SCHWERIN

This beautiful city is the administrative centre and capital of the Mecklenburg-Vorpommern region, a largely flat area devoted to agriculture and forestry and East Germany's most northern 'Land'

Schwerin Hauptbahnhof

 0700-1930 M-F

Berlin Lichtenberg 4 hrs
Hamburg 2 hrs, Rostock 1 hr
Leipzig 4 hrs

 None

 0600-2200

 0600-1930 M-F
0600-2000 Sa, Su

 None. Many imbiss near station

 0600-1930 M-F
0600-2000 Sa, Su

 24hrs

 24hrs DM 2 x 1

 At Grundthalplatz near station

 0910-1840 M-F

 24hrs

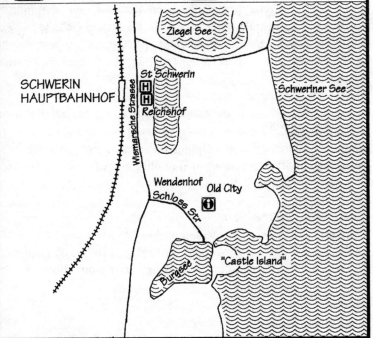

SCHWERIN HAUPTBAHNHOF

Wismarsche Strasse

Ziegel See

St Schwerin

Reichshof

Schweriner See

Wendenhof

Schloss Str

Old City

"Castle Island"

Burgsee

(state). In this area, the majority of the larger towns — Schwerin, Wismar, Rostock, Stralsund and Saßnitz — are directly on or close to the Baltic Sea. About 50km inland is what is known as the Mecklenburg Lake District, an area containing over one thousand lakes, surrounded in parts by farmland and meadows and in parts by wooded hills. The lakes offer many possibilities for recreation, although until recently these possibilities were little known outside the immediate area. The whole area is well suited to the independent traveller, although rail services could be more frequent.

The most impressive sight within Schwerin itself is without doubt the palace (Schloß Schwerin), built in the mid-19th Century on a small island in the centre of the town. Also worth visiting are the grounds of the palace with their rare trees, grotto and orangery, and the extensive Schloßgarten (palace garden) south of the island.

North of the island lies the so-called Alter Garten (old garden), a square which was once the army parade ground, and which now contains the town's theatre and museum. Many of the buildings in the old town have recently been restored, and the market square, the cathedral, the town hall and Neues Gebäude (New Building, 1783) are all of interest. At the end of one of the central lakes, the Pfaffenteich, the Arsenal resembles a white palace.

Many boat trips are available from the harbour.

From Schwerin it is easy to visit Wismar, a coastal resort on the North Sea, 30 minutes away by rail; bus services are more frequent. There are also frequent services to Rostock, one hour away, and good connections to Hamburg and Lübeck, the western German Hanseatic ports.

Tourist Information
Schwerin information is located at Am Market 11 (tel 81 23 14) and is open 1000-1800 Monday to Friday, 1000-1500 Saturday. In summer, you can take a sightseeing tour from this office or from the Hauptbahnhof.

Accommodation
Upper range
Hotel St Schwerin, Grunthalplatz 5, 2758 Schwerin (tel 52 61);
prices range from DM98 to DM265.

Medium range
Hotel Reichshof, Am Grundthalplatz 15-17, 2758 Schwerin (tel
86 40 45); rooms from DM55 to DM120.

Budget
Wendenhof, Wismarsche Straße 104, 2750 Schwerin (tel 8 34
93); rooms from DM15 to DM35, with a WC/shower on each
floor. Private rooms can be arranged via the Touristenservice —
Zimmervermittlung, MaaßKönerstraße 18, 2780 Schwerin (tel 86
57 06); prices range from DM30 to DM35.

Youth hostel
Jugendherberge Schwerin Waldschulenweg 3, 2786 Schwerin (tel
21 30 05); DM8 for juniors and DM12 for seniors. To get to the
hostel, take bus number 15 from Busbahnhofstraße and get off
near the zoo.

Camping
Check first with the tourist information office. A site exists at
Wasserwanderrastplatz, Raben Steinfeld (tel Raben Steinfeld 214),
on the Schweriner See about 2km southwest of the station. Take
tram 1 or 2 to Hermann Duncker Straße, then bus 6 to Obersdorf.

ROSTOCK

The old Hanseatic city of Rostock is the major German port on
the Baltic Sea. The old port occupies a central place at the
waterside, encircled by well preserved stone walls. These city
walls are a short walk or tram ride from the station on either side
of the Steintor, one of the ancient gates to the city. The city has
a lively atmosphere and several buildings of note, including the
Marienkirche (Church of St Mary) with its unusual astronomical
clock built in 1472.

Rostock Hauptbahnhof

0600-2145 M-F
0800-1800 Sa, Su

Berlin Lichtenberg 3 hrs
Schwerin 1 hr, Stralsund 1¼ hrs
Copenhagen 5½ hrs

Nil at station
Available through banks
and post offices

0500-2130

0600-2000 M-F
0800-1800 Sa, Su

24hrs

24hrs DM2 x 1

Opposite station

0500-2100 M-Sa

24hrs

Unterwarnow

Lange Str

Seemannshotel

H Warnow

H Steinstr

August Bebel Str

H

Gastmahl des Meeres

Am Bahnhof

Rosa Luxemburg Str

H

ROSTOCK
HAUPTBAHNHOF

Tourist Information

Rostock information is at Schnickmannstraße 13-14.

Accommodation
Upper range
Hotel Warnow, Hermann Duncker Platz 4, 2500 Rostock (tel 373 81); single from DM135 and double from DM210; the hotel is modern and central.

Middle range
Hotel am Bahnhof, Gerhart-Hauptmann-Straße 13, 2500 Rostock (tel 363 31); single from DM122 and double from DM154; opposite the station and with a good restaurant.

Budget
Seemannshotel Hans Sonne, Neuer Markt 35, 2500 Rostock (tel 371 01); single from DM55 and double from DM95 including bath and WC.

STRALSUND

Like Rostock, Stralsund is an old Hanseatic port. It is also the gateway to Rügen island, a Baltic Sea playground for sunbathers and wildlife observers. From here you can visit Sweden and Poland, or tour the Baltic coast and the Mecklenburg-Vorpommern lakes in north Germany. Stralsund is easily accessible by rail; trains from Berlin Lichtenberg take just three hours.

Accommodation
Upper range
Hotel Nord Deutscherhof, Neuer Markt 22, 2300 Stralsund (tel 3161); single from DM90 and double from DM160.

Medium range
Hotel am Bahnhof, Tribseer Damm 4, 2300 Stralsund (tel 5268); single from DM55 and double from DM115.

The Railways of Eastern Germany

by Tim Burford

In 1989 only nine of the original 47 rail links between East and West Germany remained open (two for freight only); when the borders opened there was an massive surge in traffic, but very soon a western pattern of car ownership developed in the east (after all, it was western commodities they had wanted, rather than western democracy), and now only major rail routes are to be reopened and developed. The first reopenings were on the lines between Kassel and Leipzig; three days after the border opened local DB staff took the initiative by running diesel railcars on the Walkenried-Nordhausen freight line, and in May 1990 the Eichenberg-Nordhausen line reopened.

Three more links reopened in 1991, between Bebra and Eisenach, Mellrichstadt and Rentwertshausen, and Neustadt-bei-Coburg and Sonneberg. The first of these was a restoration of the original main line via Wartha, which had been replaced in 1962 by a slower route in East German territory, via Förtha; the second was on the original Stuttgart-Würzburg-Berlin main line, although fast services will continue to run via Nürnberg or the *Neubaustrecke* (new high-speed line), and the third was a 4.3km extension to a DR junction, for largely operational reasons. Finally in 1992 another relatively minor link was due to reopen between Bad Harzburg and Stapelburg in the Harz Mountains, although this was the only project to run into planning difficulties. Most of these lines will be electrified and some will be doubled in 1994-95. The line from Helmstedt to Magdeburg and Berlin, the most important link between the two halves of the country, was electrified in 1993, bringing the two electrified systems together for the first time.

In the *Deutsche Einheit* or German Unity plan, nine of a total 17 projects are for rail infrastructure. These are, from north to south, improvements to the Lübeck-Bad Kleinem and Hamburg-Büchen-Berlin routes, a new 200km/h link from Uelzen to Stendal, and improvements to the Hannover-Stendal-Berlin, Hannover-Magdeburg-Berlin, Eichenberg-Nordhausen, and Bebra-Eisenach routes, as well as upgrading the Leipzig-Dresden line for 200km/h speeds by 1997 and building a largely new 200km/h line between Nürnberg and Leipzig. (It is also planned to introduce 160km/h tilting trains on the very twisty line between Nürnberg and Dresden.)

Additionally a *Neubaustrecke* is to be built between Hannover and Berlin, following the existing secondary line (the main line until the Second World War) via Wolfsburg and Stendal to Staaken, in the

Berlin suburbs. This will cost DM4.2bn (at 1992 values), as well as DM1.8bn for work on the approaches from Staaken to central Berlin; by 1997, 250km/h ICE trains will take just 1 hour and 45 minutes from Berlin to Hannover. At the moment, services are still slower than in the prewar days of the 'Flying Hamburger' diesel railcars.

Electrification of the eastern rail network is proceeding at a rate of c300km a year; total investment is running at DM10bn a year until 2000. The two systems, DB in western Germany and DR in the east, are losing about DM14m per year; their total debt of about DM70 at the end of 1993 has been written off by the government, and a new company, Deutsche Bahn AG, was created on January 1 1994, structured as a public limited company with a view to privatisation before too long. Already in 1993 they had a joint chairman, Heinz Dürr, based in Berlin. The most important changes are that many DB staff will lose their civil servant status, with job security and generous pensions, and that the state monopoly will be ended, with other companies having the right to operate trains on state tracks.

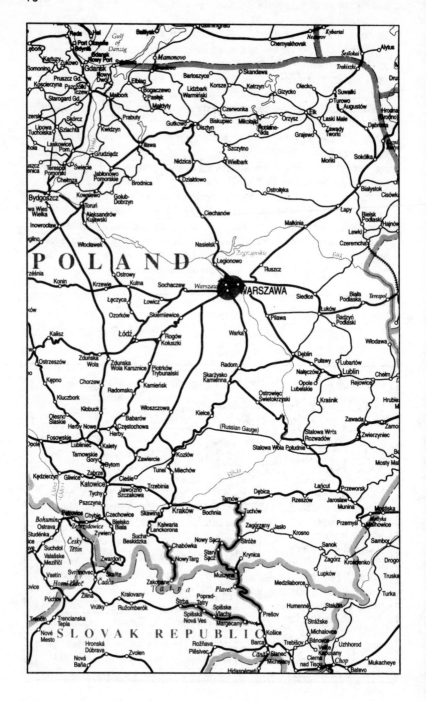

Chapter 3

Poland

Area: 312,683 km² (120,727 sq miles) Population: 38 million
Capital Warsaw (Warszawa) Population 2½m

Poland is now really open for tourist business. Visas are no
longer required of most westerners and the independent traveller
is very welcome. Package tours organised by Orbis, the Polish
tourist organisation, have been well established for years, so some
accommodation and sightseeing attractions are already in place.

Poland has had a chequered history. Until the late 18th
Century, Poland (in union with Lithuania) was one of the largest
states in Europe. However, from then until the end of the First
World War, its territory was either governed or occupied by
neighbouring states. During the interwar period, shortlived
independence returned until the Nazi-Soviet pact of 1939 put an
end to this.

The people are traditional and fiercely nationalistic, and this is
reflected in the near perfect restoration of the old town centres
and buildings, which had been destroyed by the Second World
War. Only Kraków, a superb original example of a medieval
town centre, was left untouched by the war, although the restored
towns and city centres are also well worth a visit.

Economic progress within the Comecon system was generally
slow and the country's development was hindered throughout its
period as a Soviet satellite state. Since 1989 adjustment to
democracy and the global market economy has proved difficult
for Poland's backward agriculture and industry. However,

modernisation is proceeding well and the business community is responding to the needs of the tourist, for foreign exchange is especially needed.

GEOGRAPHY

Poland is the largest of the countries covered in this book. It is more than twice the area of England and Wales and slightly larger than Italy. Except in the south, where it shares a mountainous region with the Czech Republic and Slovakia, Poland is a vast plain connecting northern Germany with the Russian steppes. However there is a rich diversity of landscape, with areas of beautiful lakes, and those searching for beautiful havens should not confine themselves to the south.

The western frontier is marked by the rivers Odra (Oder) and Nysa (Neisse), which makes Berlin a convenient gateway. Warsaw lies on the main west-east route from Berlin to Moscow, crossing the western border between Frankfurt-an-der-Oder and Kunowice, and the eastern border between Terespol and Brest. The Baltic Sea is to the north with the port of Gdańsk as a railhead. To the south west the Sudety mountains form a natural boundary with the Czech Republic, and to the south east the Carpathians form an even more impenetrable boundary with Slovakia, limiting the number of rail lines between these countries. The main international rail route to the south crosses the border between Zebrzydowice and Petrovice, on the Katowice-Ostrava route.

CURRENCY

The zloty is not a hard currency and has been subject to a decline in value against other currencies. At the time of writing $100 exchanged in Poland would make you a zloty millionaire. Anticipated devaluation may correct this anomaly at no small cost to the Polish saver, so collecting dollars and other Western currency has become a national pastime, and you can expect high purchasing power when converting from Western currencies. Be prepared for large denomination notes which are worth relatively small sums, and avoid changing too much money at one time.

WARSAW

At the centre of the country, the capital is the nodal point for its transport system, as well as the major stopping point between Berlin and Moscow; it has a scrupulously reconstructed Old Town and the main national museums and galleries.

Warszawa Centralna Station

This modern station is close to the city centre and to hotels and thus undoubtedly the best to use. Most services are available here around the clock and it is a hive of activity.

Warsaw Tourist Information Centre plac Zamkowy (Castle Square) 1/13 (tel 270 000/635 1881).
Orbis, Marszałkowska 142 (tel 276 766), open 0800-1600 Monday to Friday, produce a very good city guide in English.

Central Post Office 31-33 ulica Świętokrzyska, open 24 hours.

Banking Hours 0800 to 1600.

Accommodation
Upper range
Forum Hotel, ulica Nowogrodzka 24-26, 00-511 Warsaw (tel 210 271); single 1,000,000 zloty ($100), twin 1,200,000 zloty ($120); 751 air-conditioned rooms. When I commented to the reception manager that one had to be a millionaire to stay there, he replied, 'Nowadays, everyone is a zloty millionaire'. This is a central hotel, convenient for the station and with all the amenities associated with Inter-Continental hotels worldwide.

Middle range
Hotel Metropol, ulica Marszałkowska 99a, 00-692 Warsaw (tel 294 001), single $50, twin $80, including bath, TV and breakfast; 192 rooms, including some for non-smokers and disabled guests; near the Forum and the station.

Budget
Hotel Saski, plac Bankowy 1 (tel 201 115/204 611), single $15,

Warsaw Centralna

 24hrs

London Victoria 25½ hrs, Berlin Zoo 10 hrs,
Berlin Lichtenberg 4 hrs, Leipzig 1½ hrs,
Vienna Südbahnhof 9½ hrs, Eisenach 1 hr,
Budapest Keleti 10 hrs, Sofia 27½ hrs

 0800-1930

 0700-2200

 0630-2345 local
0800-1900 international

 24hrs

 See tickets above

 24hrs

 24hrs lower level

 0800-1400

 24hrs lower level

 24hrs

twin $26. Located on the Central station side of the old city, at the junction of Marszałkowska and Electoralna, the crescent shaped building looks imposing. Inside, you will find the rooms basic. Although they have hand wash basins, shower/bath facilities are shared and the maid will charge you for their use. Whilst the staff manner was abrupt when I visited, the charges are moderate for Warsaw.

Youth Hostels
ulica Smolna 30 (tel 278 951), often full during the season, and ulica Karolkowa 53a (tel 328 829), 2km west but also often full.

Private rooms
These are expected to increase in number. Contact Syrena at ulica Krucza 17 (tel 217 864) for bookings.

Restaurants
Al Jerozolimskie, the thoroughfare close to Centralna station leading to the river, offers several choices. At no 42, the London Steakhouse offers familiar food and jazz; try also the Passage Bar, ulica Widok 22, for food and drink at modest prices.

City Transport and Orientation
The central area of Warsaw is quite compact. It is, therefore, sensible to choose accommodation which is not too far away in order to make maximum use of your time. The old city, shopping area, parks and palaces are located on the west bank of the Wisła (Vistula) river.

Trams traverse the main thoroughfares but buses cover a wider area. Tickets for both can be purchased at the station and it is wise to buy sufficient first time, to cover all journeys. Taxis are plentiful and, like most buys in Poland, will seem good value. Walking, using a street plan, and occasional use of taxis is the least frustrating way of seeing the city.

Warsaw Excursions
Żelazowa Wola Fifty kilometres west, the birthplace of Frédéric Chopin is probably the most popular excursion from Warsaw.

Surrounded by a beautiful park, the manor house is now a dedicated as a museum to the great composer. Piano recitals are given for tourists during the summer. Coach tours are available through Orbis, or take a local train to Sochaczew and then a bus connection.

Lublin Two hours 45 minutes by rail from Warsaw, this is the largest city of the Lublin Uplands, where the land starts to rise towards the Carpathians. The route follows the valley of the Wisła and then ascends to the city. There is an old town, neo-Gothic castle, Renaissance burghers' houses and fragments of the old fortifications.

Częstochowa This town is 3½ hours by rail from Warsaw, but as most Warsaw-Katowice trains use the new Central Trunk Line there is now only one daytime train via Częstochowa, and four others terminating here. From Kraków coach travel is quicker in any case. The fortified Paulite monastery of Jasna Góra, with its mysterious icon of *Our Lady of Częstochowa*, also known as the *Black Madonna*, which is reputed to have wept during a 17th Century siege by the Swedes, is Poland's greatest Roman Catholic pilgrimage destination.

GDAŃSK

Formerly known as Danzig, this important Baltic port on the estuary of the Wisła became well known as the birthplace of Solidarność (Solidarity). It is, in fact, Poland's main seaport and an historic Hanseatic town. In the Second World War (which was sparked off here) almost the entire city was destroyed but, thanks to Polish custom, most has been carefully restored in its former style. In the old city, there is a 15th Century Gothic town hall, restored Renaissance style houses, the 17th Century Golden Gate and the huge church of Our Lady — the largest brick church in Europe. The main station (Gdańsk Główny) is located close to the old city. It is reached by hourly trains, taking 3½ hours from Warsaw.

Gdańsk

Information 24hrs

Warsaw Centralna 3½ hrs
Wrocław 7 hrs
Berlin Lichtenberg 10 hrs

None (at Hevelius Hotel below)

None

0800-1800 at kiosk outside station

24hrs
Good value soups

Reservation 24hrs

None

0800-2000 M-F
0900-1300 Sa

24hrs

24hrs

Elz

Kanał Raduni (Canal)

Hevelius

GDAŃSK
GŁÓWNY
STATION

Korzenna

Elżbietańska

Wały

Jagiellońskie

Szeroka

Church of
Our Lady

Old
City

Długa

PO

Jantar

Gdańsk Tourist Information ul Heweliusza 8 and 23, across the park opposite the station (tel 310 338 & 314 355), open 1000-1600 Monday to Friday, 0800-1500 summer weekends.

Central Post Office ul Długa 22, open 0800-2200 Monday to Friday.

Banking hours 0800 to 1700 Monday to Friday, 'best time 1000'.

Accommodation
Upper range
Hotel Hevelius, ulica Heweliusza 22, 80890 Gdańsk (tel 315 631); single $56, twin $72 (266 rooms and 10 suites).

Middle range
Jantar, Długi Targ 19, Gdańsk (tel 316 241).

Budget
Dom Turisty Miramar in Sopot (ul Zamkowa Góra 25, tel 518 011) and student houses in the university are recommended; private rooms are available from ul Elżbietańska 10 (tel 312 634), open 0700-1900 summer/1700 winter.

Camping
Brzeźno, ulica Hallera 234 (tel 566 331); category 1 — take the Nowy Port train to Gdańsk Towarowa station (one stop before Gdańsk Brzeźno), go west along ulica Uczionowska and right into ulica Hallera. The campsite (close to the beach) is marked on the left.

Gdańsk Excursions
Sightseeing cruises from Gdańsk around Gdańsk Bay and to Westerplatte.

Sopot Twenty minutes north by rail, a well known bathing resort and health spa.

Gdynia A further fifteen minutes north by rail (with trains every ten minutes between Gdańsk and Gdynia; in addition all long-distance trains from Gdańsk actually start at Gdynia), this modern city is also an important maritime centre. Delights include the museum ships *Błyskawica* and *Dar Pomorźa*, the Oceanographic Museum and Marine Aquarium and the Naval Museum.

Sztutowo Seventy-five minutes east by bus, this (known in German as Stutthof) was the first concentration camp to be built in what is now Poland, in 1939. From here a narrow-gauge steam railway runs along the coast to Stegna and then south to Nowy Dwór, a road junction for Gdańsk, Malbork and Elbląg.

Kościerzyna A railway museum is being set up here, 100km south west of Gdańsk.

Malbork This town is 40 minutes south by rail (on the Warsaw line), and castle lovers will not want to miss the sprawling castle of the Grand Masters of the Teutonic Knights, built in the 13th Century and extensively rebuilt in the 19th Century; it is one of the finest Gothic structures in Poland.

WROCŁAW

Pronounced Vratswav, and formerly the German Breslau, this city is situated on the Odra (Oder) river, in southwest Poland, and the old city, reconstructed after substantial war damage, is certainly worth a visit. Trains run both from Warsaw (some continuing into Germany or to Prague) and along the country's main cross-country axis, from Świnoujście, Szczecin (Stettin) and Poznań to Wrocław, Katowice, Kraków, Rzeszów and Przemyśl. The site had been an important fortified settlement of the Slavonic Slizanie tribe in the 9th Century. Today the city boasts several comfortable hotels and a picturesque old town area. There are numerous Gothic and baroque facades as the city has many ecclestiastical and university buildings. Lovers of culture will welcome the six theatres and nine museums. The old town is under half an hour's walking distance of Wrocław Główny station. The turrets of the station resemble those of a medieval castle.

Wrocław Tourist Information
On the corner of Rynek and Oławska; open 1000-1800 Monday to Friday, 1000-1500 Saturday.

Central Post Office
At ul Zygmunta Krasińskiego 1, east of the centre; also opposite the station and at Rynek 28, opposite Orbis main office

Banking Hours 0800-1600.

Accommodation
Upper range
Hotel Orbis Panorama, plac Dominikański 8 (tel 443 681); single $52, twin $80 (105 rooms, 8 suites). A modern hotel in the centre, close to the old city.

Middle range
Hotel Polonia, ulica Piłsudskiego 66 (tel 31021); single $23, twin $35 with bed and breakfast.

Budget
Hotel Grand, ulica Piłsudskiego 102, tel 36071, single $21, twin $28.

Hostels
Stacja Turystyczna PTTK, ulica Szajnochy 11 (tel 443 073), just south of Rynek.
Youth Hostel, ul Kołłątaja 20 (tel 38856), near the station.

Camping
Al Paderewskiego 35 (tel 484 651), to the northeast by the Olympic Stadium.

Wrocław Główny

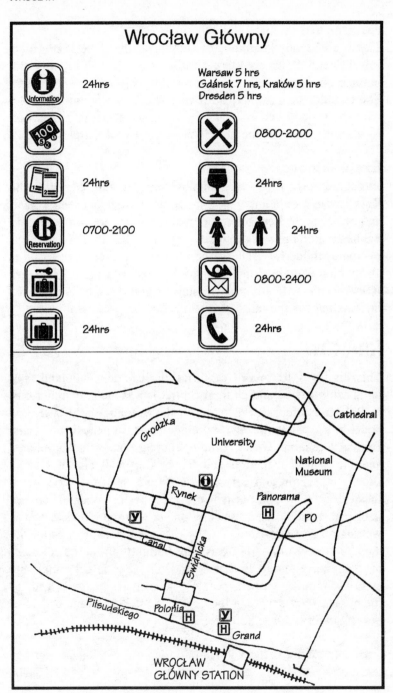

Restaurants

There are many within and amongst the hotels on ulica
Piłsudskiego. Poles tend to eat early, so expect to find, as I did,
nothing on the menu at 2130 at the Europejski Hotel restaurant.
The Grand was, however, open very late, and quite inexpensive,
with the waiters becoming as drunk as the customers. The best
restaurant in town is the Dwór Wazów at Rynek 5 (tel 441 633).

Excursions

Wrocław nestles in the Odra valley on the edge of the
Karkonosze mountains which form the frontier between Poland
and the Czech Republic; the main resorts are Karpacz and
Szklarska Poręba, both accessible by rail. The city is surrounded
by some wonderful scenery and some interesting castles, and is
also within day travelling distance, by road, of Częstochowa (*see
Warsaw* entry). If you plan to stay several days, consult tourist
information for the latest attractions.

KRAKÓW

This city was for many centuries the capital of Poland, and
remains its artistic and cultural centre. It was the only major city
in Poland to escape devastation in the Second World War, and
you can see authentic and extremely beautiful medieval walls,
Gothic, Renaissance and baroque churches and other buildings,
and the Wawel cathedral and Royal Castle. It also has some
superb museums and art galleries. Like Warsaw, Kraków is
located on the Wisła, but it is much further upstream. There are
hourly fast trains from Warsaw on the Central Trunk Line, as
well as regular departures on the east-west main line. From the
main station (Kraków Główny) head slightly to the left through
the underpass to the Barbakan and, on your left, through the
arches, the old city opens out. A grid of narrow streets leads to
the huge market square at the centre and the castle and cathedral
beyond, overlooking the river.

Tourist Information Wawel Tourist, ulica Pawia 6-8 (tel 226
091), opposite the rail and bus stations, Monday to Friday 0800-

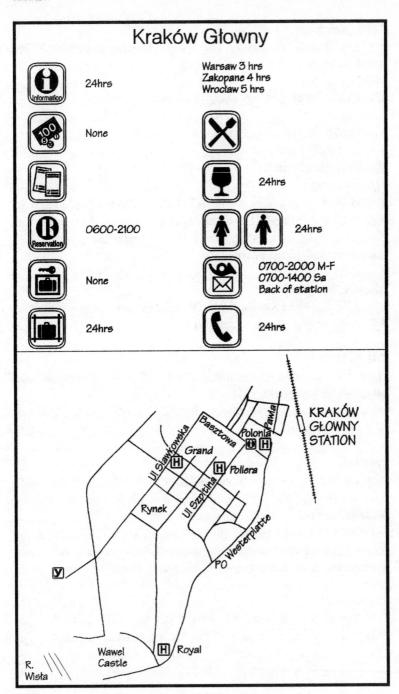

Kraków Głowny

1600, Saturday 0800-1200.

Orbis, Rynek Główny 41, 0800-1900 Monday to Friday, 0800-1300 Saturday.

Central Post Office ulica Wielopole 2.

Banking Hours 0800-1600.

Accommodation
Upper range
Grand Hotel, ulica Sławowska 5-7 (tel 217 255); single $70, twin $90 including breakfast and bathroom (105 beds). In the heart of the old city this four star hotel is very comfortable, with CTV, telephone and pleasant rooms.

Middle range
Hotel Royal, ulica Św Gertrudy 26 (tel 214 661); single $35, twin $70, with cheaper annexe behind.

Budget
Hotel Pollera, ulica Szpitalna 30 (tel 221 044), also in the old city; single $17, twin $25.
Hotel Polonia, ulica Basztowa 25 (tel 227 349); single $13, twin $19 without bath.

Hostel
Kapitol Students Hotel, ulica Budryka 2 (tel 375 989); bus 208.

Youth Hostel
Schronisko Młodzieżowe, ulica Kościuszki 88 (tel 221 951); trams 1,2,6,21 west to the Salvator tram terminus, around $2 for accommodation in a convent, but 2300 curfew.

Camping
Krakowianka, ul Żywiecka Boczna 4 (tel 664 191), bus 119 south along the Zakopane road, near the Borek Fałęcki rail station.

Restaurants

Kraków is popular with Poles as well as international tourists, and tea houses and restaurants are plentiful. For a large, traditional refreshment house try Kawiarnia Literacka, ulica Pijarska 7/Slawkowska.

Excursions
Auschwitz (Oświęcim)

The most infamous Nazi concentration camp lies about 60km west of Kraków. It can be reached by local train (generally from Kraków Plaszów station, two stops south of the main station) and is within walking distance of the station, although you may prefer a local bus or taxi. The camp remains virtually unchanged since the end of the Second World War.

Wieliczka

The Wieliczka salt mines (Kopalnia Soli) lie 12km southeast of Kraków (frequent trains, as well as tour buses), one of the largest and oldest in Europe, which have been in operation since the 11th Century. The mines are also famous for chapels carved from salt by miners over the centuries. Check with tourist information before leaving, as opening hours are restricted and the guided underground tour lasts between three and four hours.

ZAKOPANE

This town is a most refreshing centre, and Poland's best known ski resort; for the rest of the year it is popular with those who enjoy walking. It is about 100km south of Kraków, at the end of the rail line close to the Slovak border, at an altitude of 800m in the Tatra mountains. Summer is best for the independent rail traveller, as accommodation is often booked up during the skiing season.

The journey by rail from Kraków Główny or Kraków Plaszów is slow, but the scenery is far better appreciated at this pace. Spring, summer and autumn show trees and fields at their best. On the platforms, at each station, you will see a mass of cultivated flowers. After about two and a half hours, the valley narrows. Tractors give way to real horse power, there are tethered cows and strip fields, where it seems that entire families work. In another hour, a spectacular view of the Tatra mountains rises ahead.

The train slowly winds its way to Zakopane station, where wooden fences and two sets of buffers make the final stop reminiscent of seaside miniature railways.

Tourist Information Centre
Manager Ann Ritter is very helpful at Orbis, ulica Krupówki 22, 34-500 Zakopane (tel 5051) 0800-1500 summer, 2000 winter Monday to Friday, 0800-1400 Saturday; closed Sunday. Straight ahead from the station, 15 minutes walk along ulica Kościuszki, opposite the Post Office.

Central Post Office ulica Krupówki, 1000-1800 Monday to Friday, 1000-1500 Saturday; closed Sunday.

Banking Hours 0745-1200 Monday to Friday, 0745-1000 Saturday.

Accommodation
Upper range
Orbis Kasprowy Hotel, Polana Szymoszkowa (tel 4011), 4km from the station on the slope of Mount Gubalówka, single $26-40, twin $36-50; 276 rooms and 12 suites, swimming pool and night club.

Middle range
Orbis Giewont Hotel, ulica Kościuszki 1 (tel 2011), single $13-19, twin $21-33 (44 rooms, 3 suites); 1km from the station in the town centre. Residents can use the facilities of the Kasprowy Hotel; provides currency exchange and tourist information.

Budget
Warszawianka, ulica Jagiellońska 18 (tel 3261), single $5, twin $6; the reception manager apologetically commented that 'this is not a good hotel', but as viewed it would provide adequate

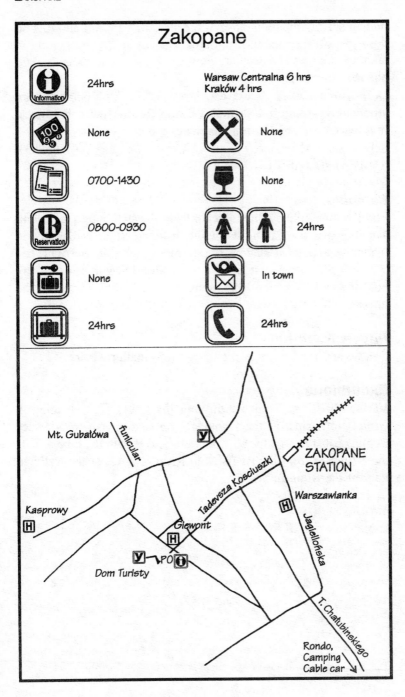

Zakopane

Information	24hrs		Warsaw Centralna 6 hrs Kraków 4 hrs
	None		None
	0700-1430		None
Reservation	0800-0930		24hrs
	None		In town
	24hrs		24hrs

Mt. Gubałówa

funicular

ZAKOPANE STATION

Tadevsza Kosciuszki

Warszawianka

Kasprowy

Giewont

Jagiellońska

Dom Turisty

PO

T. Chałubinskiego

Rondo,
Camping
Cable car

budget accommodation close to the station. Turn left and it is on
the right after a couple of minutes.

Youth Hostels
Dom Turisty, ulica Zaruskiego 5 (tel 3281), $5-8 per night; an
attractive building in a central location (behind the post office).
It is extremely popular but has many multi-bedded rooms.
Schronisko Młodzieżowe, ul Nowotarska 45 (tel 66203),
overcrowded but cheap.

Camping
Pod Krokwia, ulica Żeromskiego; from the station turn left along
Jagiellońska, then along T Chałubinskiego, right at the Rondo
(roundabout) and it's about five minutes along on the right. It's
a 2km walk from the station or the centre, but you can take any
bus towards Kuźnice (the start of the cable car into the
mountains).

Private Rooms
Can be arranged through the tourist information centre.

Excursions
Various ones are available through the Orbis TIC; sledging in
winter, raft trips on the Dunajec river and a visit to Niedzica
castle; or just head into the mountains and stay in the hikers' huts
there (details from the PTTK at ul Krupówki 12, or the National
Park at the Rondo).

Polish State Railways

by Tim Burford

The Polish State Railways (PKP) have always been relatively efficient and well-run, by the standards of the Soviet bloc. Nowadays they are modernising the system as rapidly as possible, generally aiming at compatibilty with German Railways. With a $145m World Bank loan, it is investing in the German Kurs '90 reservation system and in Austrian digital telecommunication and radio-signalling systems. Passenger services are being restructured along German lines, with the fastest expresses now labelled InterCity, and semi-fast regional services labelled InterRegio.

Under communism, the PKP both carried the average Pole 1,400km per year, the second highest figure in Europe, and also moved huge amounts of freight, in particular up to 500,000 tonnes of coal a day from the mines of Silesia to the Baltic ports (at one time moving up to 13% more than the theoretical maximum tonnage, and up to a quarter of all central and western European freight traffic). Passenger-kilometres travelled in 1992 were 37.3% less than in 1985, and freight tonne-kilometres 52.1% less, so there is now far more slack in the system. The major routes were electrified during the 1980s, and in 1984 the 233km *Centrala Magistrala Kolejowa* (CMK or Central Trunk Railway) was opened between Zawiercie (northeast of Katowice) and Grodzisk (west of Warsaw), to feed coal traffic towards Gdańsk. This also carries passenger trains at 160km/h (100mph) from Warsaw to Katowice and Kraków, so that there are now hourly InterCity services to both cities (averaging 110km/h), and the EuroCity *Sobieski* to Vienna; there is now only one day train to Katowice on the old line via Częstochowa. In addition, the LHS (Sulphur-Steel Line) was built to carry Soviet broad-gauge trains to the *Huta Katowice* steelworks.

On the main east-west route, from Berlin to Warsaw and Moscow, a new central station opened in 1974, in the tunnel built for east-west suburban services under the city 40 years earlier. After decades of carrying heavy broad-gauge Soviet sleepers (on standard-gauge bogies) from Moscow to East Berlin via Warsaw Gdańska (on the northern bypass line), a EuroCity business service was introduced in 1992 between Warsaw Centralna and Berlin, taking six hours instead of the previous seven, and as this route is also upgraded for 160km/h running, this will be further accelerated; however EuroCity-standard coaches will not be available until 1994 or 1995. Further in the future, a new high speed line is planned from Berlin to Moscow, via Poznań and Warsaw. Other links with Germany have reopened, such as that from Gorzów to Strausberg.

Main stations now have computerised ticket offices, but queueing is still a possibilty. Local tickets are only valid for the few hours after purchase, so don't buy them too soon; alternatively you may have to validate them yourself with a date-stamping machine at the entrance to the platforms. The *Polrailpass*, which can be bought from Orbis or through western agencies such as Campus Travel, is not a bargain and is only worthwhile if you don't want to buy tickets in Poland.

Fast trains are traditionally known as *pośpieszny*, marked in red on timetables, and cost 50% more than slow (*normalne* or *osobowe*) trains; it is often worth paying a bit more again for a seat reservation (*miejscówka*), although trains are not now as crowded as under communism. You must have a reservation for express (*expresowy*) or InterCity trains, marked in red with an R in a box on timetables. There are two classes, first (*pierwsza*) and second (*druga*), as well as sleepers (*miejscie sypialny*) and couchettes on long-distance overnight trains (not only from Warsaw). Although there are smoking compartments, it is usual to go into the corridor for a drag. Departures (*odjazdy*) are listed on yellow posters, and arrivals (*przyjazdy*) on white.

As in Britain and many other countries, there are moves towards separating the rail infrastructure (under a 'Railtrack'-style company) and operations, so that the later can be offered to private enterprise. Already the *Lubuska Kolej Regionala* (Lubuska Regional Railway) is operating local rail services around Zielona Góra, using second-hand Danish *Lyntog* diesel units, and resuscitated steam engines around Wolsztyn, to the east. There are proposals for a private Czech company to re-open the line from Korenov in the Czech Republic to Szklarska Poręba in the Polish Karkonosze. Most of Poland's narrow-gauge railways are now closed, but that from Rzepedź to Maidan in the Bieszczady mountains (in the southeastern corner of the country; main-line connections from Zagórz) runs a popular tourist train daily in summer.

Locomotives are classified with a simple two-letter code, E for Electric or S for Combustion, and P for Passenger, T for Freight, U for Universal, or M for Shunting. Most Polish electric locomotives are similar to first-generation BR ac locomotives, derived from the twenty EU06 3kV dc BoBos built at English Electric's Vulcan Works in Newton-le-Willows around 1960. Over 500 EU07 locomotives were based on these, and were still being ordered in 1990, together with the regeared EP08 and the articulated BoBo+BoBo ET41. Additionally over 300 ET21 and ET22 locomotives were built for freight work, although they are also seen on local passenger trains; the ET42 is a far more powerful (4680kW) class from the Soviet

Union. The 2920kW EP09 class was introduced from 1990 for 160km/h services on the CMK. The EN57 is the standard 3-car electric multiple unit, designed in the 1960s and also still being built in 1990, with a higher-powered version, the 4-car EN71, for hilly routes such as to Zakopane and Szklarska Poręba, and the EW58 high-platform version used between Gdańsk and Gdynia. New EW60 emus were to be introduced from 1990.

Diesel locomotives are mostly the Romanian-built SP32 and ST43, the Soviet-built SP44, and the home-made SP45 classes, as well as SM42 and SM48 trip shunters. Diesel railcars are rare, although some are used in the northeast.

Metros are being built in Łódź and Warsaw, but they are unlikely to open until the last years of the century.

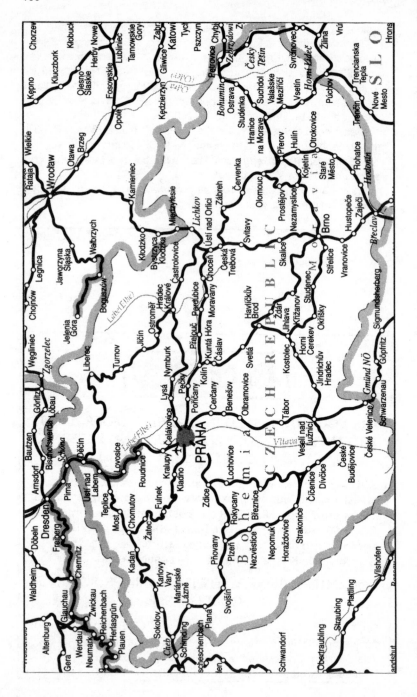

Chapter 4

Czech Republic

Area: 78,874 km² (30,453 sq miles) Population: 10,000,000
Capital: Prague (Praha) Population: 1,200,000

The Czech Republic is a largely mountainous landlocked country, bordered by Germany, Poland, Slovakia and Austria. It became part of the Federal Republic of Czechoslovakia in 1918 when the Austro-Hungarian Empire collapsed at the end of the First World War. Independence was shortlived, for in 1938 the land was once again occupied, this time by forces of the Third Reich.

Nation status was restored after the Second World War and, in 1960, the country was declared a socialist republic, although the communists had been in power since 1948. Soviet domination remained strong, as was witnessed in 1968, when the Czech uprising against repression, the 'Prague Spring', was quickly put down by Warsaw Pact armour.

Since the 'changes', known here as the 'Velvet Revolution', Czechoslovakia has witnessed the end of the 'leading role' of the Communist Party and the election of Civic Forum leader and playwright, Václav Havel as President. At the time of writing, further changes have taken place with a formal division in 1993, creating the new Czech Republic and the Slovak Republic (see Chapter 5). There have been changes, too, which more directly affect the tourist. For British tourists, a visa is not required and there is no longer a compulsory minimum currency exchange. Privatisation of state owned assets and services is proceeding at speed. This is especially true of the accommodation and money exchange sectors. In the Czech Republic, the currency is Czech crowns (Kč). At stations, it is common to be approached by enterprising individuals who will offer to change money or provide reasonably priced accommodation in private rooms.

The people of the Czech Republic are very hospitable, helpful and friendly. A good way of meeting some of them is by using private rooms from time to time. Hosts are able to accept foreign currency and often quote prices in Deutschmarks. On occasions, especially when travelling alone, you may be invited to stay as a guest with someone you meet. Your understanding of the country will definitely improve through meeting the people, as well as seeing the sights. However, such invitations are frequently spontaneous so it will depend on you how much planning you prefer to make in advance.

PRAGUE

No tour of eastern Europe would be complete without a visit to this capital city. There are good rail links, especially international expresses on the north-south run and the city serves as a terminus for many routes within the country. You will find that you can plan to arrive here at almost any time of the day, although to really appreciate the spectacular scenery from your carriage, allow for a few daylight hours when arriving or leaving.

Prague is a city of statues. Almost everywhere you look, on buildings, bridges and in squares, you will see commemorative figures. At the centre of this visual feast is the Charles Bridge (Karlův Most), one of the oldest stone bridges in Europe, which is lined with beautiful baroque statues. It is a focal point for tourists, musicians, puppet shows, artists and souvenir sellers. Fortunately, as it is a footbridge, it still retains a medieval flavour, albeit with more contemporary trading. Towering over the Charles Bridge and the river Vistula (Moldau) on the western bank, you will see Hradćany, the Prague Castle complex.

From Charles Bridge, you can reach Prague Castle easily on foot. There is so much to see here that it is very much a question of personal preference. On your ascent, you will see many attractions which will catch your eye. The area is a mass of museums, galleries and concert halls. At the castle itself, you will see ceremonial guards at the gates of the Presidential Palace. However, you are free to walk through the courtyards to St Vitus Cathedral, where Charles IV is buried.

Charles IV, King of Bohemia and Moravia, was Holy Roman Emperor from 1346 to 1378 and it is from his decision to make Prague the centre of his empire that the city achieved real significance. It was a good choice as the river Vistula, a tributary of the *Labe* (Elbe), is navigable at this point and is still used by barges today. The Gothic architectural style of some buildings, including the cathedral, originate from this great period.

Furthermore, unlike many eastern European cities, Prague remained intact after the Second World War. The legacy of old buildings and narrow streets makes the city a safe haven for pedestrians (but beware trams).

At night, Prague comes alive with many street musicians playing in the squares. The beautiful old buildings act as a spectacular backdrop to contemporary entertainment. This street life is every bit as entertaining as the more commercial tourist programmes on offer.

PRAGUE RAILWAY STATIONS

The city is served by four main railway stations.

Nádraží Praha-Holešovice

The small station north of the city which deals with many of the north-south international expresses. It is linked by tram, bus and metro with the centre.

Nádraží Praha-Hlavní

The central station, which receives some international trains (but not the *Pannonia* or *Meridian*) mainly from Vienna and Germany.

Nádraží Praha-Smíchov

Serves mainly domestic and commuter trains. You can get to Karlştejn from here.

Nádraží Praha-Střed

Primarily for domestic routes.

Blocked information is provided for Praha-Holešovice which is the least central of the four but it is likely to be the one which most eastern Europe rail travellers will use.

PRAGUE HOLEŠOVICE

Tourist Information Centre

Čedok, Nám Příkopě (between metro stations Nám Republiky and Můstek). Very well organised for information, currency exchange, rail enquiries, excursions and visitor service reception desks for respective countries with most languages spoken. Open 0800-1800 Monday to Friday; 0800-1230 Saturday.

General Information

Pražská Informační Slušba (PIS), Prague 1, Nové Město, Na Příkopě 20 (tel. 54 44 44).

Main Post Office

Open 24 hours, Nové Město, Jindřišská 14, Prague 1, 24 hour service and poste restante service.

Urgent Accommodation Service

Čedok accommodation Panska 5, until 2000 Saturday and until 1800 Sunday (tel 225657).

Accommodation

Upper range

Hotel Palace, Panská 12, 110 00 Prague 1 (tel 219 7111, 236 0008, 235 9394), single from US$230, twin US$265. Central, air conditioned, minibar, excursions.

Middle range

Europa, Václavské 25, Prague 1 (tel 236 5274), from single US$100; twin US$150. A lovely piece of Art Nouveau (1904). On Wencelas Square in the heart of Prague.

Prague Holešovice

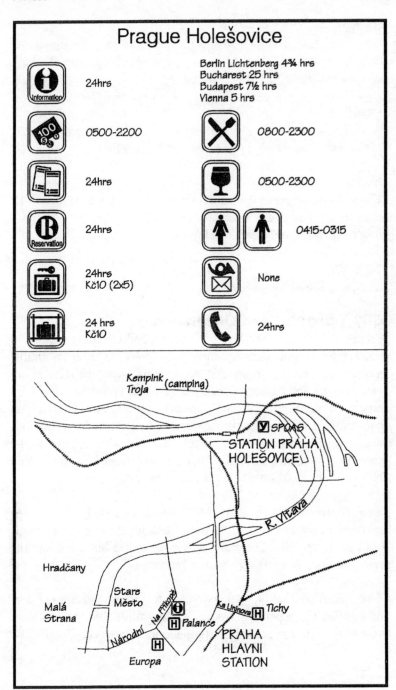

24hrs

Berlin Lichtenberg 4¾ hrs
Bucharest 25 hrs
Budapest 7½ hrs
Vienna 5 hrs

0500-2200

0800-2300

24hrs

0500-2300

24hrs

0415-0315

24hrs
Kč10 (2x5)

None

24 hrs
Kč10

24hrs

Budget
Hotel Ariston (formerly Tichy), Seifertova 65, Kalinova 65, Prague 3 (tel 6278840), from single US$40; twin US$60. Restaurant, close to Hlavní station.

Pension
Private rooms available from Seacom in Holešovice station from 26DM (tel 216 15 33 3) or Čedok at Nové Město.

Hostel
Youth Hostel Spoas, Jankovacova 63A (631 804891), from $8 each in a 6 bed dorm with kitchen, TV, showers, 0100 curfew. Just over the flyover east of Holešovice.

Camping
Kempink Troja, Trojská, 10 minutes from Holešovice by 112 bus.

City Transport and Orientation
Prague is quite a small city so, with a good town plan, much is accessible on foot. Obtain a town plan (*plán města*) from almost any tourist service or news-stand, costing about 10 Kčs. Many news-stands and station buffets will also sell you tickets valid for bus, tram and metro, priced 4 Kčs per journey. At this price you can afford to buy a stock. Remember to cancel the ticket in a machine, as inspectors do check. Locals who appear to be travelling buckshee generally have a season ticket. Routes should be clearly marked on the town plan.

The Metro operates until 2400. It is extremely fast, quite modern, noisy and difficult to find. Look for small green symbols with the letter 'M'. There are only three routes but these link the rail stations and most city tourist locations.

The Tram service is extensive, easy to follow and a good way of sightseeing, especially from the river. With a good town plan, you will have no problem getting about.

Buses cover every part of the city. The sights are not as visible as from a tram and you may need to rely on the driver or a friendly passenger to locate your stop.

Boat Trips
The river is not exploited as much as in many cities. Čedok tend to organise evening cruises along with other day trips and excursions by coach. For example, you may take an evening cruise for three hours from 1900 which includes food, music and dancing for 550 Kčs.

A daytime boat tour from the pier just south of Jiráskuv Most costs 30 Kčs but heads south away from the more interesting sights. If you desire a quiet (no commentary) view of the outer suburbs, parkland and a road bridge, this will suit you.

Restaurants and Eating Out
There is an impressive choice of places to eat and you should have no trouble selecting somewhere to suit your pocket and taste. Prices here are low, so even those on a tight budget will eat and drink well. The largest concentrations of restaurants, taverns (*bierstuben*) and wine restaurants (*weinstuben*) are in three central areas; Stare Mesto, Nove Mesto (the streets adjoining the Vltava) and Mala Strana (the streets west of the Charles Bridge going up to the Hradčany). *Weinstuben*, as their name suggests, do not serve beer but offer a large choice of wines. The wide variety of food on offer is familiar and acceptable to the English palate. Try, for example, Beograd, Prague 2, Vodičkova 5 or U Šuterů, Prague 1, Palackého 4. £3-4 will buy ample food and drink.

Bierstuben are almost as numerous as *weinstuben*. They often have a Bavarian flavour with long trestle tables in the garden. The beer is Czech, given that Pilsen and Budweiss are brewed nearby. At *bierstuben*, you can choose from *steins* or smaller quantities of dark or pale beers. Perhaps the most famous, especially with Germans, is U Fleků, Prague 1, Křemencova 11, but U Supa, Prague 1, Celetná 22 is also worth a visit.

Remember that many restaurants start to close at 2200 so eat early to avoid disappointment and allow some queuing time at the more popular hostelries.

Prague Excursions

Coach trips organised by Čedok will save you time but, obviously, there is a cost involved. Rail travel, and ordinary bus, for that matter, is still very cheap, but you will need to either plan well or allow time to use a combination of local trains, buses and footwork.

Karlştejn Founded in 1348 by Emperor Charles IV, this fortress served as a stronghold for the imperial regalia. Its location, just outside Prague, and its historic associations, make this fortress extremely popular and worth a visit. The villagers amply provide for the visitors' eating, drinking and shopping requirements, from their gardens bordering the tourist trail. Rail from Nadraží Praha-Smíchov 30 minutes, 16 Kćs return, then 30 minutes walk.

Karlovy Vary (Carlsbad) — Prague 4 hours
One of the most famous spas in Europe. A largely 19th Century town with the other main spas of Mariánské Lázně (Marienbad) and Františkovy Lázně (Franzensbad) nearby (but too far for a day rail trip from Prague). A place to watch the waters being taken and to move back a century. Probably best to leave from Prague Holešovice before 0900 for a scenic trip allowing plenty of time for the return journey to Prague.

Pilsen (Plzeň) — Prague 2 hours
A beer drinker's Mecca, complete with beer sampling in the Prazdroj Beer Hall and a brewing museum. The town is of little merit architecturally. Trains leave from Praha Hlavní station.

Brno Prague 4 hours (see Brno section below).

České Budějovice
Lengthy rail route, better to go on a bus excursion. Like Pilsen, a place of pilgrimage for beer drinkers. Home of the famous lager, Budweiser Budvar. You will also see one of the largest squares in Europe, dominated by the Samson fountain.

BRNO

With a population of 400,000, Brno is the second city of the Czech Republic. The capital of Moravia, it is not as well known as Prague. Only at times of exhibitions does it really have some of the cosmopolitan flavour one might expect.

It dates back to the 11th century and developed around the Špilberk Castle rock area. This lies at the edge of the centre of the city, now surrounded by a large park. Unfortunately, the castle, completed in 1287, is undergoing restoration and has been closed for a number of years.

The city below has some interesting old streets and squares, particularly Freedom Square with its Renaissance and baroque buildings, and the Cathedral of St Peter and St Paul is worth a visit, as is the very colourful outdoor cabbage market. You can also visit the exterior of the castle.

Accommodation
Upper range
Grand Hotel, Třída 1. Máje 18-20, 65783 Brno (tel 23526), single 1775 Kčs ($53), twin 3,020 Kčs ($90) with breakfast. Close to station, Čedok tours leave from here.

Middle range
Hotel Metropol, Dornych 5, 60200 Brno (tel 337114-5), from 900 Kčs ($27). Near to station but further away from town.

Budget
Hotel Avion, Česká 20 (tel 4221 5016/4232 1303), doubles without showers from $19, with showers from $38 including breakfast. An architectural monument by the 1920s functionalist architect Bohuslav Fuchs.

Pensions
Consult Čedok or try Pension Miron — from station tram 1, 7, 11, 18 direction Řečkovice, get out at fifth stop, Hrnčířska, turn right along Rybniček for 300 metres.

Brno

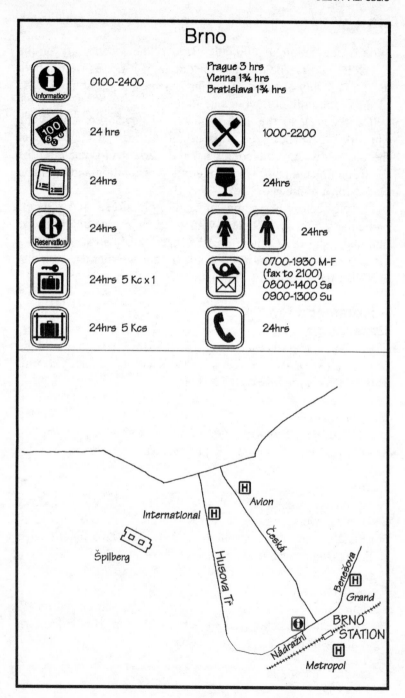

Camping
Cho Obora by the lake, by 10, 3, 18 tram, then bus.

Restaurants
A better and ever increasing choice. Head for the city centre. San Marco near Stredova behind the International Hotel is a good bet. For 100 Kčs (about £2) you will eat well including wine.

The Railways of the Czech and Slovak Republics

by Tim Burford

Czechoslovakia was an artificially constructed country, put together from the remains of the Hapsburg and German empires after World War I, and this origin is still reflected in its railways. Some routes are electrified at 3kV dc and others at 25kV ac, and many routes still seem to be heading for Vienna, Budapest or Berlin, regardless of the present frontiers. These border crossings were largely disused during the Cold War, but are now being reopened and upgraded, with the main lines from Prague to Vienna via Gmünd and to Dresden via Děčín being electrified, as well as other links from Bratislava to the Hungarian border, from Ostrava and Prešov to the Polish border, and from Breclav to Bernardsthal in Austria. Again, the "Velvet Divorce" of the Czech and Slovak Republics has led to further dislocation; previously, the main route through Slovakia was that from Prague to Košice via Poprad, carrying freight on to the Soviet Union, but now the line from Bratislava to Košice must take its place.

Nowadays the Czech Republic is far more go-ahead than Slovakia, and this is reflected by their respective railways, although both are planning to invest and to extend electrification. On July 1 1994 Czech Railways (CD) was split into operations and infrastructure divisions, along the lines required by the EU; CD is no longer the sole operator, so that the 20km line from Korenov to Szklarska Poręba (in Poland) may be taken over by the Jizera Railway, and the Velké Brezno-Zubrnice line by Czech Commercial Railways. Administrative posts have been cut by 20%, while 160km/h routes are to be developed from the German and Polish borders to the Austrian and Hungarian borders. Additionally 3.4bn Kčs is to be invested in new motive power, with new diesel multiple units needed to replace locomotives on minor lines and new multi-voltage electric locomotives for international expresses. Fortunately Skoda, one of the world's best locomotive manufacturers and supplier of most of the Soviet Union's ac express locomotives, is based in Plzeň, so that there are no problems finding hard currency to import new locomotives. Most will be 200km/h developments of the successful Cl.499 series, as well as the fifteen 4000kW machines of Cl.372 built in 1991 for Berlin/Dresden-Děčín-Prague trains, as well as a possible "tribo" (three bogie) 6000kW design.

There are now InterCity and EuroCity services from Prague to

Berlin, Warsaw and Vienna, and phones are to be introduced on all main lines. One the freight side, daily intermodal services are to run from České Budějovice to Villach in Austria, and from Lovosice to Dresden, across a border where there are often thirty-hour delays for trucks at the road crossing.

Prague's Metro dates from 1974 and is reputed to have been built largely by political prisoners, quite plausibly as it is a clone of that in Moscow; the 40km network is still growing, with line B being extended to Českomoravská in 1991, to Zlicin in 1993 and to Pocernická in 1995. Currently the metro carries 1.3m passengers a day, 35% of the city's public transport traffic, and this is to rise to 50% by 2000. The other main means of transport is by tram, and again it is fortunate that CKD Tatra, manufacturer of one-third of the world's 70,000 trams, is based in Prague. The German company AEG is to invest DM100m for a 55% stake in CKD, now selling a modern low-floor design which is replacing older trams in Prague, and a 65km/h triple-unit found in most of the cities of eastern Germany.

Slovak Railways (ZSR) has fewer resources for new investment, but there is still much of interest here, including a broad gauge (1524mm) line from the Ukrainian border to the steelworks of Košice, and the metre-gauge rack-and-pinion lines (built in 1896, closed in 1932 and reopened in 1972) from Poprad and Štrba to the Tatran resorts of Tatranská Lomnica, Starý Smokovec and Strbské Pleso. In Bratislava a metro is planned under the Danube to the huge and ugly Petržalka housing development on the south bank.

THE GLOBETROTTERS CLUB

 An international club which aims to share information on adventurous budget travel through monthly meetings and *Globe* magazine. Published every two months, *Globe* offers a wealth of information from reports of members' latest adventures to travel bargains and tips, plus the invaluable 'Mutual Aid' column where members can swap a house, sell a camper, find a travel companion or offer information on unusual places or hospitality to visiting members. London meetings are held monthly (Saturdays) and focus on a particular country or continent with illustrated talks.

Enquiries to: Globetrotters Club, BCM/Roving, London WC1N 3XX.

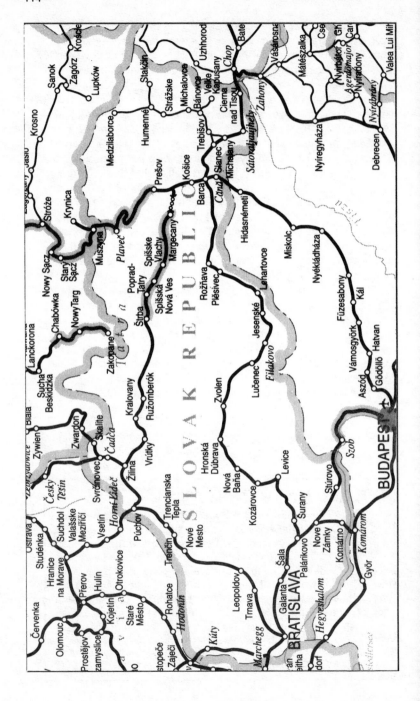

Chapter 5

Slovak Republic

Area: 49,035 km² Population: 5,000,000
Capital: Bratislava Population: 450,000

Note that there is now a separate Slovak currency, the Slovak crown (SK).

BRATISLAVA

The capital of Slovakia, Bratislava is described in tourist literature as 'a pearl on the Danube'. It is in the west of Slovakia at the edge of the Carpathian Mountains and occupies, with Vienna, the gap between these mountains and the Alps.

As a settlement on the Danube, Bratislava has been inhabited for at least 1600 years. In the 16th Century, it became the capital of Hungary (as the Turks were then occupying Budapest) and, in 1969, the capital of Slovakia within the Federal State of Czechoslovakia. In 1993, with the division of Czechoslovakia, Bratislava became the capital of the newly-created Slovak Republic.

The city has good rail links with Prague, Vienna and Budapest. During the season (usually May to September) you can go by boat from Bratislava to Budapest and Vienna too. This does, however, depend on the level of water in the Danube and sometimes it is necessary to travel part of the distance by bus. Tickets are available from the port office of Danubia where the boats leave (Fajnorovo nábrezi).

From Prague, you skirt the hillside above the Danube to arrive at Bratislava railway station, which is above the city. The forecourt is a mass of *imbiss*, trams and buses with no sign of the city centre itself. Do not be deterred, it is below you, but you will need to use some form of transport to arrive there unless you prefer a 30 minute walk.

NOTE This is a perfect centre for seeing parts of Hungary and Austria. Both their capitals are within easy reach. If you decide to stay here, where it is much cheaper, you will make substantial savings on accommodation.

Bratislava Hlavni
Accommodation
Upper range
Hotel Forum, Mierové Námestie, 81625 Bratislava (tel 348111), from single $150, double $225. New, luxurious, a 10 minute walk from station and centre. Many ladies of the night in the foyer.

Middle range
Hotel Devin, Rázusovo Nábr, Bratislava (tel 330851), single $82, with extra bed $114 (no doubles as such), including breakfast. Old, traditional, comfortable hotel overlooking the Danube. Service generally good.

Budget
Hotel Carlton, Hviezdoslavovo Námestie, Bratislava (tel 335141), single $25, double $40. Central, in need of refurbishment, slow and poor service. (Closed for refurbishment, early 1994.)
   Hotel Lux, Šafárikovo námestie (tel 55471). East of the Hotel Devin (above) and just north of the bridge.

Youth Hostel
Sputnik Junior Hotel, Drieňová (tel 234340), 180 Kčs (£3.50/$5-6) per head. Located on the edge of the city (tram 8 from station) near a lake, this is primarily for students and young people. Show an international youth card. Very comfortable accommodation with en suite facilities; restaurant, buffet and disco at extra charge.

Bratislava Hlavná

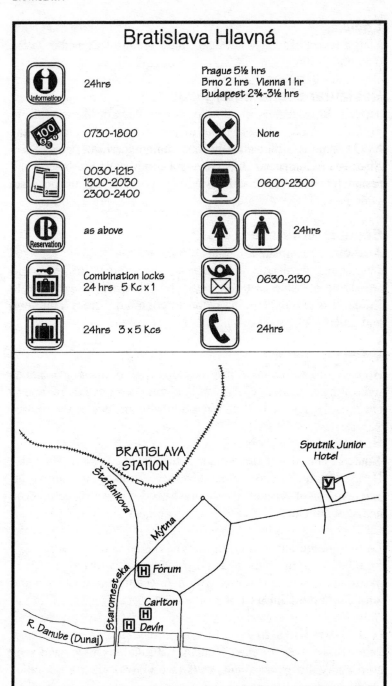

24hrs

Prague 5½ hrs
Brno 2 hrs   Vienna 1 hr
Budapest 2¾-3½ hrs

0730-1800

None

0030-1215
1300-2030
2300-2400

0600-2300

as above

24hrs

Combination locks
24 hrs   5 Kc x 1

0630-2130

24hrs   3 x 5 Kcs

24hrs

BRATISLAVA STATION

Sputnik Junior Hotel

Štefánikova

Mýtna

Staromestska

Fórum

Carlton

Devín

R. Danube (Dunaj)

Camping
Zlaté Piesky, also by a lake 8km out — tram 4 from the station or tram 2 from town.

Restaurants and Eating Out
The city is extremely good value for money and there is plenty of variety. You will not be out of pocket dining in many of the hotel restaurants. For a really interesting experience, go to Stara Sladovňa (Cintorínska 32). Here is a complex of beerhouses and restaurants both inside and out with a variety of live music. Take your pick!

Some Excursions
Trenčín — Bratislava 1 hour 40 minutes
The town is north east of Bratislava in the Váti Valley. You will see the impressive castle as you approach the town en route to Žilina. It is still undergoing reconstruction but there is a museum and gallery.

Vienna — 1 hour
An easy run which takes just over one hour by train. It is not as interesting as using the Danubia boat but does leave more time to see the city, and arrives at Wien Südbahnhof, nearer the centre.

Budapest 3-3½ hours
You cross the flatter flood plain of the Danube towards Hungary. If you can, make one journey via Nové Zámky and Štúrovo, as you will travel through the Danube bend and valley before you arrive at Budapest.

Győr (pronounced Dure) — 2 hours
Equidistant from Bratislava and Budapest, this town has a good example of a baroque centre with many churches and a cathedral containing the gold bust of St Ladislaus.

Rail Tour Itinerary
From Bratislava, you pass Trenčín, with its lofty tower and keep surrounded by palaces and walls (see above). The Váti Valley

begins to narrow some two hours later, industrial Puchov appears and the real treeline begins, together with a glimpse of the river amidst the modern blocks. Chalet style villages made up of houses with high pointed roofs and balconies take over.

From Žilina, the landscape becomes even more 'alpine' for the train moves through the river valleys below the High Tatra mountains (second highest in northern Europe after the Alps).

From the top of the valley, the route passes several lakes, surrounded by forest and villages. The journey is naturally slow, given the gradients, but it gives ample time to appreciate some wonderful views. On the left, the barren tops of the Tatras can be viewed before Štrba. Half an hour later, now six hours into the journey, the modern industrial town of Poprad Tatry looms into view. (Connections here for mountain railways to the Tatra mountains — see Košice excursions).

From Poprad Tatry, the route follows the Hornád valley. The slow, scenic descent completes the seven hour journey to Košice. It is a very memorable experience.

KOŠICE

At the centre of the rail network in the east of the Slovak Republic lies Košice, with a population of about 250,000. It lies in the valley of the Hornád river and is the administrative centre of eastern Slovakia.

Košice has yet to be flooded with tourists. It retains a quiet charm which complements its rural location. The old city, with its university buildings and cathedral, gives the impression that little has changed over the centuries. The main street, currently known as Leninova, is pedestrianised. It contains numerous cafes and restaurants behind beautiful facades.

The determined rail traveller may be interested to know that this could be the base for visiting four other countries. The borders of Poland, the Czech Republic, Ukraine and Hungary are all within about two hours train ride. However, the rail link with Bratislava is not as short, so be prepared for a lengthy, although picturesque, journey.

Košice

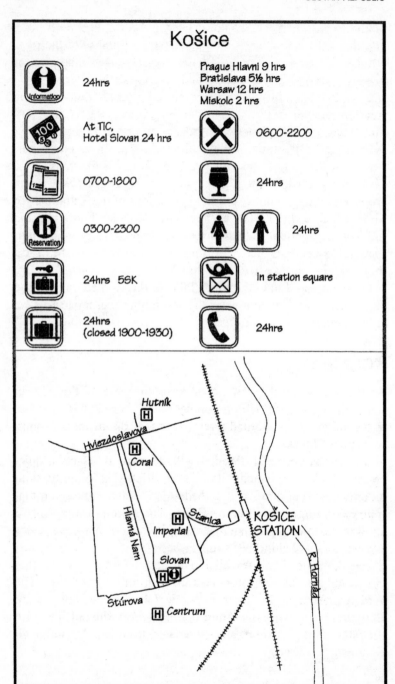

Information	24hrs		Prague Hlavni 9 hrs Bratislava 5½ hrs Warsaw 12 hrs Miskolc 2 hrs
	At TIC, Hotel Slovan 24 hrs		0600-2200
	0700-1800		24hrs
Reservation	0300-2300		24hrs
	24hrs 5SK		In station square
	24hrs (closed 1900-1930)		24hrs

Hutník

Hvlezdoslavova

Coral

Hlavná Nam

Stanica

KOŠICE
STATION

Imperial

Slovan

R. Hornád

Stúrova

Centrum

Accommodation
Upper range
Centrum Hotel, Sovietskej armády, Košice (tel 768206). The newest and most luxurious in town.

Middle range
Hotel Slovan, 1 Rooseweltova, Košice (tel 27378), single $31, double $47 including breakfast.

Budget
Imperial Hotel, Mlynska 16, Košice (tel 22146), single $12, double $17. Hotel Hutník, Tyršovo Nábrežie 6, Košice (tel 37780), single $9, double $12. Very comfortable and helpful, considering the price.

Hotel Coral, 04001 Košice, Kasárenskènam 5 (tel 26095), single $7.50, double $9. Fairly new, private, looks like good value.

Camping
Autokamping (Salaš Barca), Alejová (tel 58309). Bus 8 to Alejová.

Restaurants and Eating Out
For Košice it is early days to emulate the more popular destinations but this does mean that almost all the hotel restaurant prices are modest. The main street, Vlisa Hlavna, contains many fast food and other outlets. For a friendly wine bar, try Vinareň pri 'Fontaine', Hlavni ul 57. At night, you might like to join the young people of Košice, and promenade along the street and see the fountain dancing to recorded music. Close by are the gothic Cathedral of St Elisabeth and the Town Hall, both currently undergoing restoration.

Excursions
Poprad Tatry and the Tatra Local Railways 1½ hours
At Poprad Tatry, you can head up to the mountain resorts on mountain railway journeys ranging from 15 minutes to 90 minutes. At Štrba, you can take a rack railway to Štrbskè Pleso

or return this way back to Košice. Refer to the Thomas Cook European timetable for more details.

Caves

Eastern Slovakia has the majority of impressive caves in the country. Several are easily accessible from Košice but they are easier to reach by road. To prepare yourself, request the booklet *Caves in Slovakia* from your local Čedok office.

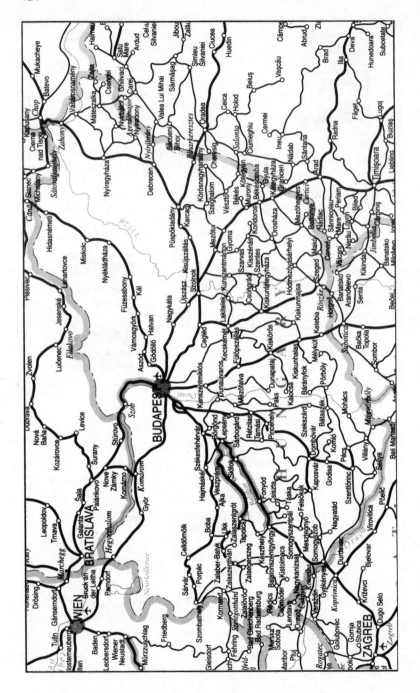

Chapter 6

Hungary

Area: 93,030 km² (35,919 sq. miles) Population: 10,600,000
Capital: Budapest Population: 2,000,000

The Republic of Hungary stands as the crossroads of central
Europe. Whilst it is small in terms of area and population, the
country is well prepared to welcome visitors and transit
passengers. This policy is reflected in relaxed border formalities
at customs and passport control. Since 1991, it has not been
necessary for UK citizens to obtain a visa and the Hungarian
authorities are keen to abolish visa obligations with many other
countries (check with their embassy).

At present, Hungary is the most advanced of eastern European
countries in catering for all types of tourist. Whilst it is still
inexpensive by western European standards, it is more expensive
than its neighbours and in its hotel industry tries to emulate the
quality and standards of Austria. Austrian and other western
European companies have now significant stakes in Hungarian
hotel businesses.

As a small country with a centrally located capital city, it is
inevitable that transport facilities converge on Budapest. This is
especially true of the rail network which links every major
destination with the capital. There are now no internal air links
so the national air carrier MALEV now operates only from
Budapest airport. Lack of air transport has placed a greater
emphasis on the rail service. Rail travel is quite comfortable and
relatively fast due, to some extent, to the flat terrain.

BUDAPEST

For any extended rail tour of eastern Europe, the city of Budapest is unavoidable. Almost every international express stops here, whether from Berlin, Prague or Warsaw to the north or from Romania and Bulgaria in the south. With such very good rail links, the city is a good place to begin or end a tour.

International trains arrive and depart from three Budapest stations. Keleti (eastern) is the largest but you may also find yourself using Nyugati (western) and Déli (southern). They are all linked by the metro but this section will treat them separately for block information purposes.

Budapest Kelenföld, a major suburban station, is a stopping point for most trains to the west and vice-versa. The Hotels Wien and Rubin are just 200m from here using the rear entrance of the station. There is also some budget accommodation north of the Wien in the form of pensions and private rooms.

Budapest offers history, modern shopping facilities, entertainment and a variety of thermal baths, some dating back to Roman times. The old settlement of Buda on the west bank includes the old city with the citadel at its summit. IBUSZ (the state tourism company) produce excellent guides to the area. On the eastern side of the Danube is the Pest part of the city. Most hotels, restaurants, shops and commercial premises are to be found here. Although the central area is not too large, use of public transport will make movement less exhausting and prices are still quite low.

Budapest Keleti
Tourist Information Centre

With accommodation and foreign exchange service at Keleti. IBUSZ, Petöfi Tér 3, 24 hours, exchange, private rooms, accommodation, information 118-9775 IBUSZ, Josef Attila 18; office hours for hotel rooms, currency, train tickets, etc.

Central Post Office, Petöfi Utca, 0800-1800 Monday to Friday, 0800-1300 Saturday.

Budapest Deli

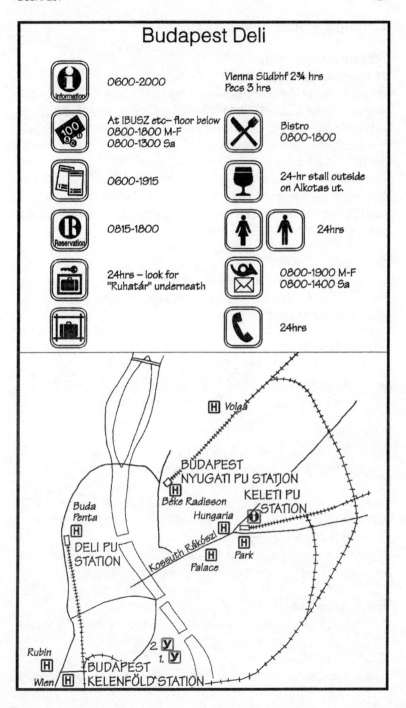

0600-2000

Vienna Südbhf 2¾ hrs
Pecs 3 hrs

At IBUSZ etc— floor below
0800-1800 M-F
0800-1300 Sa

Bistro
0800-1800

0600-1915

24-hr stall outside
on Alkotas ut.

0815-1800

24hrs

24hrs — look for
"Ruhatár" underneath

0800-1900 M-F
0800-1400 Sa

24hrs

Volga

BUDAPEST
NYUGATI PU STATION

KELETI PU
STATION

Béke Radisson

Buda
Penta

Hungaria

DELI PU
STATION

Kossuth Rákóczi

Park

Palace

Rubin

Wien

BUDAPEST
KELENFÖLD STATION

Banking Hours 0800-1700 Monday to Friday.

Accommodation
Upper range
Grand Hotel Hungaria, Rákócze út 90 (tel 1229 050) — opposite station; 220DM single, 270DM twin with bath and breakfast; extremely comfortable and luxurious. Travel office with exchange.

Middle range
Palace Hotel, Rákóczi út; single from 50DM, twin 80DM, without bath/shower. Friendly staff, central location, some rooms with bath/shower. Travel office with exchange. Rates expected to rise commensurate with refurbishment.

Budget
Park Hotel, Baross Tér 10 opposite station. Two star status, from single 50DM, double 80DM. Rates could rise significantly. Quality poor at time of visit.

Youth Hostel
1. Bog Dánfy u, adjoining Irinyi Jozsef u (below).
2. Irinyi Jozsef u (in Buda) from 20DM per person per night.
Or contact Express Central Reception (tel 166 5460).

Camping
None near station, although there are many good ones throughout the country. Information and publications from Danube Travel Service (see *Useful Addresses*) or MCCC (Hungarian Camping and Caravanning Club), Customer Service Office, Budapest VIII, Üllői ut 6 (tel 133 6536, telex 22 6927) or Tourinform, Budapest V, Sütő u 2 (tel 117 9800).

One convenient site is at the Római-Fürdő stop on the HEV local rail line from Batthány tér north to Szentendre.

Budapest Déli
For many local departures south and west and some to Vienna.

Accommodation
List for Buda side of the city (consult also other station blocks).

Upper range

Hotel Buda Penta, 1012 Budapest, Krisztina Krt 41-43 (tel 156-6333), from single 180DM, twin 240DM, close to station, sauna, solarium, fitness room, swimming pool, night club.

Middle range

Hotel Rubin, 1118 Budapest, Dayka Gábor u 3 (tel 185 0192), from single 105DM, 150DM twin. South west of city, this apparthotel is a good 30 minutes on bus 139. Although a little remote, swimming pool, sauna, solarium, various sports and breakfast are included.

Budget

Hotel Wien, 1118 Budapest, Budaörsi út 88-90 (tel 166 5400), from single 65DM, twin 75DM. Again, south of city, trolleybus 139 to/from Déli — horse-riding and nightclub. Also access by rail from Budapest Kelenföld (see above introduction to Budapest).

Youth Hostels

See Keleti.

Camping

See Keleti.

Budapest Nyugati

This is Budapest's west station but it is to the north of the city centre. It was designed by the office of Gustave Eiffel in 1874.

Accommodation
Upper range

Béke Radisson Hotel, 1067 Budapest, Teréz (Lenin) Krt 97 (tel 132 3300), from single 270DM, twin 330DM. Near to the station; swimming pool, sauna, solarium, fitness room and night club.

Middle range

Volga Hotel, 1134 Budapest, Bózsa Gy. út 65 (tel 129 0200), from single 100DM, twin 140DM. Two stops north on the metro, close to Danube and spas, nightclub.

Budapest Nyugati

 0600-2000

Bratislava 2¾ hrs, Cluj 8½ hrs,
Prague & Polesovice 8 hrs,
Debrecen 3 hrs

 At City Tourist office
on Platform 10
0800-1800

 Also McDonald's and
24-hr shop

 0530-1800

 0800-1800

  24hrs

 Next to station

 24hrs,
next to platform 10

 24hrs

Budapest Keleti

 0700-1800

London 27 hrs, Berlin Lichtenberg 14 hrs
Prague Holesovice 7½ hrs, Bucharest Nord 14 hrs
Vienna Westbahnhof 3½ hrs, Sopron 3 hrs,

 0700-2100

 0700-1800

 Back of waiting room
24hrs   3 x 20 Fts

  24hrs

 24hrs 60 Fts

 24hrs at back of station

 24hrs

 24hrs

Budget
See Keleti.

Youth Hostels
See Keleti.

Camping
See Keleti.

City Transport and Orientation
The central area of the city on either bank of the Danube is where the majority of tourist locations are and there is a good public transport network. In high summer, around one million tourists are added to the two million population of metropolitan Budapest. This can present a mobility problem.

It should not be necessary to buy maps or other information, as Hungary is very tourist friendly and most literature is available free. It comes in publications of the Hungarian Tourist Board, from IBUSZ offices or Budapest tourist offices (at all three stations) and, also, from hotel group publicity in the larger hotels.

Ask especially for: the booklet *Travel in Hungary* which has a good section on Budapest; *Programme in Hungary* — a what's on guide; *Budapest — A practical guide for young people*; *IBUSZ — Guaranteed Programmes*, which also includes bus tours and has a useful map in the centre.

Tickets
Most continental city transport systems appear to be much more trusting than those in Britain. Passengers in eastern European cities are generally expected to buy tickets and validate their own, usually through some sort of machine. Given that many locals purchase period passes, the process may not become immediately apparent to the short term visitor. I met numerous travellers travelling without tickets and some actually thought transport was free! None of these transport systems are free and I can vouch that inspections do take place. By Western standards, fares are low and more easily affordable for tourists than locals. To ensure that fares remain modest and to travel without guilt, it is sensible

to try and understand the charges levied. An information extract
from the Budapest Transport Company in 1991 will serve as a
guide.

TRAVEL INFORMATION for bus, tram, trolleybus, underground,
cogwheel and suburban railway passengers. You must buy your ticket or
pass before you travel.

Tram ticket costs 12Ft valid for trams, trolleybuses, underground,
cogwheel railway and suburban railway within the Budapest area.

Bus ticket costs 15Ft valid for buses.
After boarding trams, buses, trolleybuses, trains of suburban railway, M1
underground line and cogwheel railway, please validate your ticket by
inserting into a cancelling machine. On the M2 and M3 underground
lines, you must insert your tram ticket into a canceller at the barrier. Your
cancelled ticket is valid for one hour and for one travel only. For transfer,
please use new ticket. If you change to another line, you have to use
another ticket. Remember to keep your ticket until you leave the
destination station.

You can buy tram and bus tickets only in advance at the booking
offices of BKV, the ticket offices of underground, cogwheel and suburban
railway stations, terminals, from automatic vending machines, in tobacco
shops, post offices, on railway and country bus terminals, at the Ferihegy
airport, travel agencies and from vendors.
   One day passes are also available (no photocard required) which give
you unlimited travel on public transport vehicles shown on them from
0000 to 2400 hours on the day stated.
   Bus one day pass costs 120Ft.
   Tram one day pass costs 96Ft.
   They can be purchased at
   - the ticket offices of the underground stations,
   - the ticket offices of the suburban railway stations Batthyáy tér, Margit
hid, Árpád hid, Római fürdü (Szentrendre Line), Örs vezér tere (Gödöllö
Line) and Vágóhid (Ráckeve Line),
   - the booking offices II., Moszkva tér. V., Felszabadulás tér, Akácfa
utca 15, VII., Baross té, VIII., Kálvin tér, IX., Boráros té, XI., Móricz
Zsigmond körter, XIII., Rajik László utca 2., XIV., Bosnyák tér and XIV.,
Mexikói út.
Under 6s can travel with you free.
   Passengers evading fares responsibility and offending against travel
conditions must pay penalty fare.

Amount of fine: 400Ft on the spot, increasing by 1300Ft in case of failing
to pay within 30 days.

You can travel without any extra charge if you have no more than two
pieces of luggage the size of each not exceeding 40×50×80cm.
Budapest Transport Company (BKV)

Underground — Metro
There are three metro lines and they cross at Deák Ter (Square)
station. Tourinform, the Budapest tourist information office is
located here, at Sütö u (tel 117 9800). Deli, Keleti and Nyugati
railway stations are all linked via the Metro, which runs from
0430 to 2310.

Bus
Budapest city buses are navy blue and manufactured by the
famous Hungarian Ikarus company. The stops usually have maps,
the route, the names of the stop and the freqency. 'É' attached to
the number of the bus indicates a night service.

Tram
The horse-car, a service which dates back to 1866, was the
predecessor of today's electric street cars in Budapest. Twenty-
one years later horse power was replaced by electricity by which
the street cars and suburban trains have been powered ever since.
To mark the centenary of the introduction of electric street cars
Budapest Transport Company restored three old vehicles which
date back to the early years of this century. They are now
operated during the course of the tourist season between Margit
híd and Nopráaros tér (Margaret Bridge and Boráros Square) on
the line of tram number 2 on the Danube's left embankment, and
on the opposite embankment on the line of tram number 19,
between Batthyány tér and Móricz Zsigmond kötér (Batthyány
Square and Zsigmond Móricz Circus).

Funicular Railways
Here is yet another alternative. The third *cograil* in Europe was
built in the Hungarian capital city in 1874 and only Switzerland
and Vienna were ahead of it. You can enjoy a magnificent

panorama of the Buda Mountains from the cars working their way uphill from Márosmajor to Széchenyi hegy (Hill).

Built on the east side of Castle Hill, the *funicular* is something you must try if you want to enjoy a good ride and have a pleasant view of the variety of buildings erected east of the Danube. Constructed in 1870, it was destroyed completely during the siege of Várhegy (Castle Hill) in the closing stages of the First World War. In 1987 it was rebuilt to the original design. The lower terminal is at Clark Ádám tér (Adam Clark Square) close to zero milestone near the tunnel under the Hill, reached by tram number 19 or buses numbers 4 or 86.

The upper end of the funicular is close to the Royal Castle from where you can walk to Mátyás *templom* (Matthias or Coronation Church), Halászbástya (Fishermen's Bastion) and the Hilton Hotel in just under 10 minutes.

Taxis
These are plentiful but, given the congestion, not particularly fast. They contain meters but the road system ensures that most routes are not direct. Use with discretion.

Restaurants and Eating Out
As befits an extremely popular tourist city, Budapest has a wide choice of places to eat to suit every taste and pocket. Space does not permit an extensive coverage of what is available but there are many within walking distance of Deák tér metro station. Pick up a copy of *Programme in Hungary*, a monthly what's on guide, published for the Hungarian Tourist Board.

Eating after about 2200 on Sundays can be a problem for many restaurants close early. One restaurant where you can eat really late with modest prices is Trojka on Andrássy south of Octogon; Greek and international food with a lovely atmosphere.

Selected Excursions
Szentendre and the Danube Bend
If you ask any local about what to visit near Budapest, the answer will nearly always be Szentendre. This lovely artists' village is popular with tourists and is the home of the famous Kovács

Margit Ceramics Museum. It is a very rewarding day visit.

How to get there:

Train from Batthyány tér 40 minutes — Szentendre station about 20 minutes from the village. Very frequent service and cheap.

Boat with IBUSZ, a nine hour tour including Szentendre towards Visegrád and the actual 'bend'. Includes lunch, cocktails and dry snacks — Wednesday, Friday, Saturday, 1 May — 31 October, 74DM, £25+.

Coach with IBUSZ for 10 hours. Includes the three main centres of Szentendre, Visegrád and Estergom — Tuesday, Thursday, Saturday, 1 May — 31 October. Price as boat.

Lake Balaton — (2½-3 hours — Budapest Déli)

The largest fresh water lake in central Europe can be reached by bus excursion or train. The main rail route follows the southern side of the lake through Siófok, Fonyód, Balatonszentgyörgy to Keszthely, while a minor line follows the north side to Tapolca. The southern side is lined with beach resorts, while the north side is more historic.

Pécs — (Budapest Deli 2½-3 hours)

Pécs (pronounced Paitch) lies in the south of Hungary close to the Croatian border. It is sheltered by the Mecsek hills and the city goes back to Roman times (see the Archaeological Museum). It is a treasure trove for those who love architecture with many periods represented, including Medieval, Turkish and baroque. The journey from Budapest is essentially rural with an undulating landscape until you pass Dombóvár, when the train begins a steeper climb across the Mecsek.

Debrecen — (Budapest Nyugati 2½ hours)

Most of the journey crosses the Great Plain. Unless you enjoy a largely flat arable landscape, you will find the trip disappointing. The third city of Hungary has little to attract the visitor either. It is more suitable for an hour or so stopover than a special day excursion.

Miskolc-Tiszai

0340-2315

Budapest Keleti 2½ hrs
Eger 2 hrs   Debrecen 2 hrs
Košice 2 hrs

0900-1930

0600-2100

24hrs

24hrs 3 x 20 Ft
in underpass

0800-2000 M-F
0800-1400 Sa
0800-1200 Su

As above

As above

0400-2300
in underpass

24hrs

MISKOLC-GÖMÖRI
STATION

Pannonia
[H]

Bajcsy-Zsilinszky Endré út

Barcoss Gabor V

R. Szinva

Széchenyi Istvan VT

MISKOLC-TISZAI
STATION

Hámor [H]
Miskolc-Tapolca
(Camping)

MISKOLC
(Budapest Keleti 1¾ — 2¼ hours)

The second city of Hungary does not look impressive from the station but it has an historical centre with pedestrianised area and painted houses. The first part of the journey is through a very picturesque region but, beyond Hatvan, the line crosses the northern part of the Danube plain. The surrounding area of Miskolc has much to offer, especially the wine areas of Eger and Tokaj but this is not feasible in a day excursion from Budapest as well. The main station is **Miskolc Tiszai**.

Tourist Information Centre
Széchenyi u. 3—9 (tel 18291), open 0800-1630, 0800-1300 Saturday.

Central Post Office Széchenyi, closed Saturday and Sunday.

Banking Hours 0800-1700 Monday to Friday

Accommodation
None near the station — walk or tram 31 to the city centre.

Upper range
Hotel Pannonia, 3525 Miskolc, Kossuth L, utca 2 (tel 329811), from single $31, double $41, with shower. Very comfortable, exceedingly cheap for a 3-star — prices lower outside summer.

Middle range
Hámor Hotel, 2525 Miskolc, Széchenyi u 107 (tel 353617). A smaller 1-star hotel, very central with good facilities, pets allowed. From around $9 without breakfast for a single or double 'actually less than my room in a pension' (Tim Burford, 1994).

Budget
Fenyö Panzió, 3519 Miskolc, Görömbölyi u 85/A (tel 66241), five rooms, comfortable small pension.

Camping

Éden Camping, 3515 Miskolctapolca, Károlyi M. út 2 (tel 68421); just outside the city to the south, very well equipped but only 100 spaces.

Sightseeing

Although Miskolc is an industrial city, it contains a number of beautiful parks and good shopping facilities. Climb the hill up to the TV tower to get a panoramic view. It is a perfect centre for exploring this lesser known region.

The following excursions should be considered:

Eger The southwest — with castle, cathedral and baroque architecture. Home of the famous Bulls Blood wine.

Tokaj To the east — small village from which the famous sweet wine gets its name.

Aggtelek The north — here, as part of a party, you are able to explore the extensive cave system, some 22km long. An opportunity to look at many colourful stalactites.

All the above are reached more easily by group tour although you can get by rail to Eger with one change at Jüzesabony.

SOPRON

Budapest Keleti 3 hours, Wien Südbahnhof 2 hours

The journey from Keleti begins by crossing the Danube. The landscape is undulating to Tata and you will see picturesque homes and churches sprinkled up the hillside. Passing Komarom at the edge of the Danube, you arrive at Györ (pronounced Dure), which is worth a stop for its architecture. The final hour to Sopron is over fairly flat terrain with a mix of woods and farmland. The final minutes are very attractive, through a valley with neat rows of grape vines. On arrival, you will not be disappointed by the historic town centre.

A Hungarian border town with Austria where the station has a comfortable 'International Waiting Room', for the semi-independent Györ-Sopron-Ebenfurth line for which Inter-Rail is also valid. The atmosphere encourages a 'stopover', although it's possible to make a day trip from Budapest.

Tourist Information Centre In station, open 0800-1900
daily; very helpful.

Central Post Office Open 0800-2000 Monday to Friday,
0800-1200 Saturday.

Banking Hours 0800-1200 Monday to Friday.

Accommodation
Upper range
Hotel Lövér, H-9400 Sopron, Várisi utca 4 (tel 11061), single
$44, double $58. Situated on the edge of the town in beautiful
rural surroundings.

Middle range
Hotel Palatinus, H-9400 Sopron, Új utca 23 (tel 11395), single
$21, double $44. Central with indoor swimming pool.

Budget
Hotel Pannonia, H-9400 Sopron, Várkerület 75 (tel 12180),
double $27, double $35 with bath, no singles. Not so cheap but
the town is popular — a very central location.

Camping
Lövér Camping, 9400 Sopron, Pöcsi-domb (tel 11715). Large site
with capacity for 1050.

Sightseeing
Esterhazy Chateau
Forty minutes by bus from the town. The baroque summer palace
of Prince Nicolas Esterhazy and its grounds are open to the
public.

Hungary's Railways

by Tim Burford

Hungary lies at the heart of Central Europe, with Budapest just 250km east of Vienna, and the main line between these two cities is set to become one of the main links between east and west. It is planned to spend £117m on upgrading the Hungarian section for 160km/h running (currently the maximum is 140km/h), and £167m on 160km/h rolling stock (the first being delivered in 1994); additionally OBB (Austrian Railways) is building dual-system Cl.1014 locomotives, based on the standard Cl.1046. In 1990 there were 800,000 passengers a year on this route; there are now a million a year, and this is expected to rise to 2.4m by 1995 and even more in 1996 when Budapest will host the World Expo, even though the upgrading is unlikely to be complete by then. Before 1989 there were just four trains each way per day, taking three hours, and there will be ten each way, including EuroCity expresses, taking two hours.

Overall, passenger numbers are falling, although average journeys are getting longer, so that passenger-kilometres travelled in 1990 were 16% higher than in 1985 at 11,298m. Freight traffic has fallen to 87.4m t, 25% less than in 1985, and tonne-kilometres are also in decline; however, with economic recovery, traffic is expected to grow in 1994, despite a 20% rise in tariffs. Nevertheless, major transformations are under way, with a bill passed in late 1993 to split the MAV (already converted into a state-owned company, as opposed to a government department) into a *Railtrack*-style infrastructure division and an operating division, and to remove its monopoly; its workshops are to be sold off. In 1994 the government is to allow Ft 21.4bn investment, almost as much as in 1992 and 1993 together. Ft 4.5bn has been allowed for redundancy payments; the workforce was cut from 113,000 to 78,000 in 1992 by early retirement, and this is to fall further to 70,000 in 1994.

MAV needs to replace its aged and underpowered diesels, and 537km (notably from Miskolc to the Slovak border at Hidasnémeti and from Přspökladány to the Romanian border at Biharkeresztes) are to be electrified by the private sector over the next four to five years. In addition EBRD money is being sought to restore the 22.5km link to Murska Sobota in Slovenia. Hungary was at the forefront of the development of electric traction, with industrial frequency (25kV 50Hz) main-line electrification since 1932, and Ganz-Mavag, the long-established Hungarian manufacturer of electric trains, is now thriving under the ownership of the Leeds company Hunslet. Since 1988 it has been supplying electric multiple units with modern three-phase traction to MAV, and is now producing a 160km/h version for semi-fast InterRegio services, as well as prototype suburban emus.

There are other problems; Serbia owes Ft 5bn, and a crime wave has led to cables being stolen and batteries being removed from level crossing signals, leading to Hungary's worst traffic accident on 12 February 1993, when eleven children were killed in a school bus hit by a train.

One oddity is the Györ-Sopron-Ebenfurth Railway (GySEV), an independent system owned 44% by the Hungarian state, 42% by MAV, and 14% by private shareholders; this crosses the border into Austria, which provides a subsidy and may also take a stake in the GySEV. Cross-border traffic is expected to rise four-fold by 2000, so the track is to be doubled and 25kV electrification extended, with ex-MAV V43 electric locomotives replacing Soviet-built M62 diesels, and railcars being used for passenger traffic.

Budapest's metro is the oldest in continental Europe, with the Millenium line opened in 1896, commemorating the foundation of Hungary in 896. This was followed in 1950 by the east-west line 2 and in 1976 by the north-south line 3. A fourth line is planned but is unlikely to be ready for the 1996 Expo, despite political pressure. In 1993 the Budapest Transport Association (BKSz) was created to coordinate metro, bus and rail services, including the HÉV, a network of local railways dating from 1902, of which that from Batthyány tér north to Szentendre is the most useful for visitors. There is also a funicular from Clark Ádám tér up Castle Hill in Buda, and another from Fasor ut to Széchenyihegy, where it connects with the Pioneer Railway, an overgrown toy-train system which winds through the Buda Hills to Hűvösvölgy — well worth a ride!

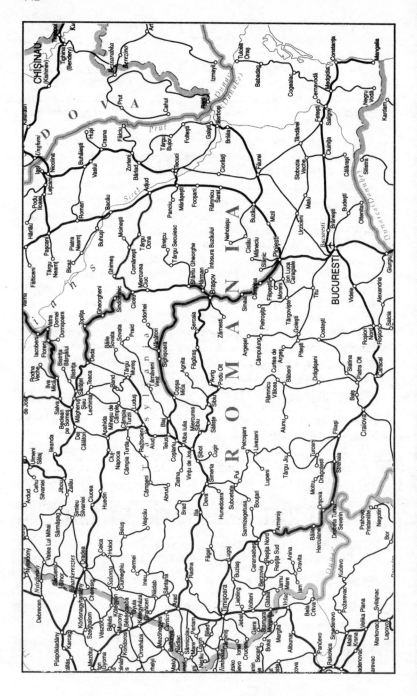

Chapter 7

Romania

Area 237,398 km² (91,699 sq miles) Population 23 million
Capital: Bucharest (*Bucureşti*) Population 2 million

Romania is probably the least known of our eastern European states. Much more than in Bulgaria, independent travel has been discouraged. Those who have visited the country are likely to have been package tourists to the Black Sea coast or skiers in Transylvania. As a rail traveller, you have the opportunity to travel where few Western people have gone before.

One of the latest to join the Inter-Rail scheme, Romanian Railways (*SNCFR Societatea Naţională a Căilor Ferate Române*, often just known as the CFR, pronounced ChéFéRé) are enthusiastic that potential customers do not use their system just for transit. The country is almost the size of the United Kingdom and it is covered by an extensive, if slow, rail network. Although Bucharest serves as the hub of this network, it is a long way from the geographic centre of the country and direct cross-country connections are possible as well.

POLITICS

No introduction to Romania would be complete without some comment on recent history and politics. In 1947 the country became the Romanian People's Republic following the abdication of King Michael. Rule by the Romanian Communist Party continued in 1965 when Nicolae Ceauşescu became leader. As

President of the State Council from 1967, and 'elected' president from 1974, he came to rule the country with an iron rod with the aid of his 'security' forces, the Securitate. Estimates vary but as many as one in three Romanians may have become informers at this time. Adjustment to a freer society has been difficult.

Unpopular programmes up to 1979 included restrictions on foreign travel, political and cultural repression and severe rationing of food and fuel. Economic policies were designed to pay off the national debt by denying goods to the population and exporting them. An additional policy, called systematisation, which aimed to level villages and replace them with apartment blocks, was seen by some as the final straw.

In mid-December 1989 violent demonstrations in Timişoara spread across the country. The army defected to the new political leaders of the National Salvation Front (FSN) but there was still direct opposition from the Securitate. This bloody episode moved towards conclusion with the execution of Ceauşescu and his equally hated wife Elena on Christmas Day 1989.

After this an interim government reversed most of the unpopular former policies, and elections were held in May 1990 and September 1992. The more progressive market orientated opposition coalition proved too much for many rural voters, who re-elected former communist Ion Iliescu and his allies; most educated urban people now speak of the 'so-called revolution', as the FSN is seen as merely a new generation of communists with a different label. However a gradual approach to economic reform and the transfer of ownership is in progress. Continued state ownership of hotels fosters a 'gradual approach' to service.

THE PEOPLE

Despite the freedoms now granted, Romanians are still strongly influenced by the past. A secret police still exists, and people will warn you that mail from abroad will be opened. International letters to and from Romania can take anything between five days and over one month, which seems to confirm this. This will rarely put them off making contact with you but do not ignore their concerns. For example, if they suggest you should not take photographs, do take notice.

Train travellers have about the best opportunity to make contact with local people. Currently you are a rare commodity and, after so many years of isolation, they are curious. English speakers are highly prized and you will frequently be asked for your address. At present, Romanians cannot get visas for western countries without invitations. Obtaining foreign currency is a second obstacle for them, so expect a period of correspondence before you can show them your homeland. They will, however, be wonderful hosts to you.

LANGUAGE

Romanian is the official language, a Romance language with many archaic forms and admixtures of Slavonic, Turkish and French words. If you have some knowledge of Latin, Italian, French or Spanish you should at least be able to understand most notices. Hungarian and (decreasingly) German are spoken in border areas and amongst the ethnic minorities. French has been the second language taught in schools but English is fast becoming the popular choice.

GEOGRAPHY

Natural barriers form most of Romania's frontiers. The river Danube forms most of the southern border with Bulgaria, and the Black Sea (to the south) and the river Prut (to the north) form the eastern border with the former Soviet republics of Moldova and Ukraine. The Ukrainian border then crosses the Carpathian mountains due west to the Hungarian plain. The western border with Hungary and Serbia bulges out a little from the Carpathians, giving Romania some good lower lying agricultural land. The most fertile land is Wallachia, along the Danube to the south, Moldavia, to the east of the Carpathians, and Dobrogea (or Dobrudja), the coastal strip. Otherwise almost half the country comprises the high ground of Transylvania and the Carpathians.

The varied natural landscape is complemented by a diverse built environment. Contrary to popular opinion, many towns have retained their older buildings and there are many beautiful villages in the north. Regrettably, the same cannot be said of the coastal developments.

CURRENCY

The leu (lion) is not a hard currency but is now used for most transactions. Hotels now display their room tariffs in lei rather than in US dollars or Deutschmarks (although Romanians pay about a fifth of the displayed prices).

The export of lei, other than very small amounts, is viewed as a serious matter, and it is likely to be confiscated at the border; in any case you cannot change lei abroad. As you will find that a little buys a lot here you should change only small quantities of money, as required. Bring some money in travellers cheques for security, and also plenty of low denomination dollar bills. Inflation is high and consumer prices increased 200% in 1992, with similar annual rises predicted. This is reflected in all lei priced tariffs. The steady depreciation of the leu renders any attempt at accurate pricing difficult. £1 bought around 100 lei in 1991, whereas in summer 1993 official rates reached 1,200 lei. The accommodation categories are a useful guide with many cheap rooms in the $7.50-$15 band.

BUCHAREST

The city may have been known as the 'Paris of the East' until the 1930s, but this is hard to believe nowadays. Certainly the buildings and nightlife do not live up to this accolade, although in the construction of massive boulevards Ceauşescu may have been emulating Baron Haussmann in Paris, as well as Kim Il Sung in North Korea. This project has certainly caused similar destruction, and Bucharest, unlike Paris, still bears the scars. This is particularly visible in the area east of Piaţa Unirii, facing Ceauşescu's former palace, which with its rusted cranes and half-built towers could pass for a shipyard. Go there on a Sunday to see the fountains along Bulevard Unirii, the road leading to the unfinished palace.

The city lies in the middle of Wallachia on the banks of the river Dimbovița, a sub- tributary of the Danube. Bucharest was of little significance until around 1330, when Vlad the Impaler (also known as Dracula) built a citadel against the Ottoman Turks, and it was not until 1659 that it became the capital of Wallachia, finally becoming capital of Romania in 1861. It has suffered disasters of natural and human origin, which have left few good examples of architecture of any period; nevertheless the building profile is largely low and there are many large parks to enjoy.

Tourist Information Centre
Bdul Magheru 7, Bucharest (tel 6133 915) hours 0800-2000 (only exchange after 1700)

Very helpful, stock a book of the last 100 days of Ceaușescu. Call for car rental, accommodation in all Romania, excursions, exchange, train and plane tickets.

Central Post Office Calea Victoriei, Bucharest, hours 0700-2000.

Banking Hours 0800-1200.

Accommodation
Note Expect far higher prices than those shown below as a result of inflation and market positioning. Dollar prices will be a better guide than lei.

Upper range
Hotel București, Calea Victoriei 63-81, Bucharest (tel 6154 580), single from $107, twin from $150. This centrally located prestigious hotel, built in 1982, has swimming pools and an ice cream salon which is a favourite treat for local people.

Middle range
Athénée Palace Hotel, Str Episcopiei 1-3, Bucharest (tel 6140 899), single from $25, twin from $30, colour TV and bath, breakfast extra. This ornate building is reputed to be the oldest and (once) classiest hotel in town, now being refurbished as a 5*

Bucharest (Bucureşti Nord)

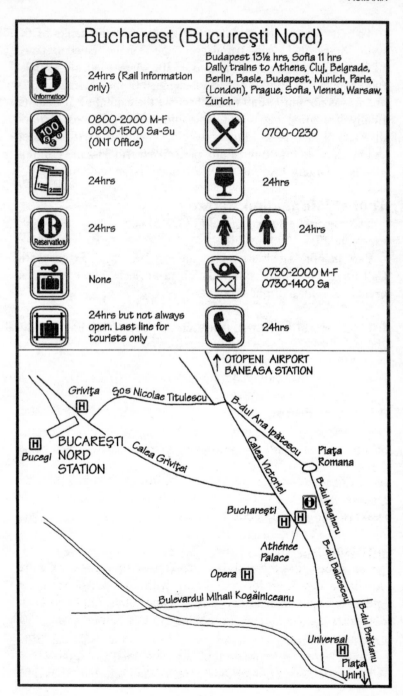

Information — 24hrs (Rail information only)

Budapest 13½ hrs, Sofia 11 hrs
Daily trains to Athens, Cluj, Belgrade, Berlin, Basle, Budapest, Munich, Paris, (London), Prague, Sofia, Vienna, Warsaw, Zurich.

0800-2000 M-F
0800-1500 Sa-Su
(ONT Office)

0700-0230

24hrs

24hrs

Reservation — 24hrs

24hrs

None

0730-2000 M-F
0730-1400 Sa

24hrs but not always open. Last line for tourists only

24hrs

OTOPENI AIRPORT
BANEASA STATION

Griviţa   Şos Nicolae Titulescu

B-dul Ana Ipătescu

BUCUREŞTI NORD STATION

Bucegi

Calea Griviţei

Calea Victoriei

Piaţa Romana

B-dul Magheru

Bucureşti

Athénée Palace

B-dul Balcescu

Opera

Bulevardul Mihail Kogălniceanu

Universal

B-dul Brătianu

Piaţa Uniri

Hilton, after which its prices will certainly be over $100.

Clinica Geriatrica (2km from Otopeni Airport), $65 including all meals (1993).

An unusual alternative recommended by traveller David Cole of Edinburgh. A chance to experience life in a partly converted geriatric hospital, keen to accept tourists. It is ably run by manageress Daniella Cordieu. A twin room 'not overdecorated' includes TV, refrigerator, bathroom with shower and bath and a veranda. Meals, which you share with the geriatrics, are described as adequate. The hospital grounds are surrounded by fields.

Budget

Hotel Grivița, Calea Griviței 130, Bucharest (tel 6505 380), single from 9,000 lei ($9), twin from 15,000 lei, also 3 and 4 beds. Close to the station, with 101 beds.

Hotel Bucegi, Str Witing 2, Bucharest (tel 6375 225), prices as Hotel Grivița, basic WHB, B+W, view of the station.

Hotel Opera, Str Brezoianu 37, Bucharest (tel 6141 075), single from 31,000 lei ($16), twin from 49,000 lei, $30 (1994), nearer the centre.

Hotel Universal, Str Gabroveni 12, Bucharest (tel 6148 533), 3,500 lei per person, central but very basic, with toilet and bathroom on each landing. It is used for student accommodation most of the year.

Private rooms

Tourist Information Centre will advise, from $10 to $15 (plus $2 commission to TIC). Often hosts will collect guests, include breakfast and provide good facilities.

Sightseeing

For an overview of the sights, the Tourist Information Centre provides a city tour for four hours with an English speaking guide. Pick-ups can be arranged from some hotels. Exploration on foot or by taxi (negotiate for a half day) can be fun. Use a TIC map for planning.

Some sights are accessible by the Metro, Bucharest's underground rail system, such as the Village Museum (Şos

Kiseleff 28), which is open 1000-1700 daily. This is located in the Herăstrău Park (metro Aviatorílor), one of the most pleasant areas of the city. It is probable that exhibits in the History Museum of Romania (Calea Victoriei 12, 1000-1800, except Mondays) will change and that the Art Gallery (Str Ştirbei Vodă 1-3, 1100-1800, except Mondays and Tuesdays) will show more than the two rooms of drawings which were the only displays when I visited. There are many more museums, such as the Natural History Museum (Şos Kiseleff 1), the George Enescu Museum of Music (Calea Victoriei 141) and the Bucharest Municipal History Museum (Bdul Brătianu 2), as well as the Curtea Veche (Old Court) at Str Iuliu Maniu 31, and lots of small Orthodox churches, mostly from the 18th Century and often tucked away behind more recent buildings.

CONSTANŢA

This ancient city is the focal point of Romania's coastal region, Dobrogea. It is a port, close to the canal which links the Danube with the Black Sea. Constanţa retains much of its Roman heritage with monuments scattered around, and the remains of the Roman docks and its preserved mosaic must be seen. These are visible from the narrow streets of the old city.

The main line from Bucharest to the coast is immensely busy in the summer, so that you should be prepared to queue a long time for tickets at Bucharest and even to stand all the way to Constanţa. There are also summer-only trains to Mangalia from most of the major towns of Romania.

Tourist Information Centre
Expected to open in 1992 at end of station, but still unopened (0600-2000). Hotels currently provide the service.

Hotel Continental Information Bureau, Bdul Republicii 20 (tel 615660), is very helpful. Take trolleybus 40, 42, 43 or taxi ($1) for currency exchange and excursions, open 0900-2100.
Palas Hotel, Str Opreanu 5 (tel 614696) for exchange and excursions, open 0900- 2000.

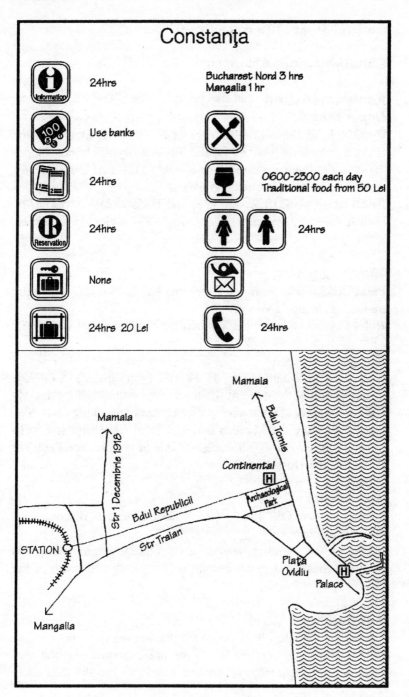

Constanţa

Information — 24hrs

Bucharest Nord 3 hrs
Mangalia 1 hr

Use banks

24hrs

0600-2300 each day
Traditional food from 50 Lei

Reservation — 24hrs

24hrs

None

24hrs 20 Lei

24hrs

Central Post Office Bdul Tomis.

Banking Hours 0800-1200.

Accommodation
Upper range
Hotel Rex, in the centre of Mamaia beach resort 6km north of Constanţa by trolleybuses 41 and 50, is now widely considered the best. Go there for a drink or a meal as the staff are generally attentive and the live music is pleasant.

Parc Hotel (tel 831326, 831197) and Perla Hotel (tel 831670), both at the south end of Mamaia, single $27, twin $35, breakfast extra.

Middle range
Palas Hotel, Str Opreanu 5, Constanţa (tel 614696). Good value, traditional menu, TV, shower.

Hotel Continental, Bdul Republicii 20, Constanţa (tel 615660).

Budget
Hotel Apollo, Mamaia (tel 83 18 16), twins from $15 (1993). Seaside hotel at the edge of the resort. Well furnished rooms. Mr and Mrs Marga, the managers, offer concessions on production of this book. Take the Mamaia bus 32R from Constanţa station to the end of the route. Walk back a couple of minutes and the hotel is next to the Hotel Siret.

Apartments
Tourist service 'OK' (tel 23 07 10) from $5 to $10; discounts for 10 days or more.

Out of the summer season, good quality accommodation is available cheaply at many coastal resorts, north and south of the city.

Sightseeing
Constanţa is a good base for exploring Roman ruins both in the old city and further afield. There are museums of National History and Archaeology, Art and Geology, and the Romanian

Naval Museum. There are also various buildings such as the Aquarium which exploit the city's long marine associations.

The coastal railway from Constanţa south to Mangalia passes through many of the more popular seaside resorts, with stations at Eforie Nord, Eforie Sud, Costineşti and Neptun. However, for beach and sea lovers, a 20 minute bus ride north to Mamaia gives the easiest access to an inviting sandy coast.

Heading north from Constanţa by rail involves taking a local train via the junction of Medgidia, 35 minutes to the west, to Tulcea. This journey takes at least four hours each way and is not comfortable for a day trip (although the day coach tours are worth considering). Even an overnight stop in Tulcea allows only minimal time to explore the delights of the nature reserves of the Danube delta — but take powerful mosquito repellant. Tulcea Tourism Agency, Str Isaccei 12 (tel 11607 or 14720) provide advice and authorisation for access to the reserves for independent travellers.

SUCEAVA

Note Suceava has two stations, of which Nord is the more important: double check before leaving.

Suceava is in the north eastern corner of Romania, close to the border with the former Soviet Union, now independent Ukraine and Moldova. This most important rail route links Bucharest with Kiev and Moscow. Standing on the platform at Bucureşti Nord, you cannot fail to notice the sturdy coaches (built to the Soviet broad gauge) which need to withstand hostile weather and long distances.

Depending on your preference, you can choose between day time trains for a view of the landscape, or a night ride to arrive refreshed in Suceava early the following morning. The southern part of this route is flat and not especialy scenic, so you could sample a cabin in a sleeping car on the Istanbul to Moscow *Sofia Express*, now using Bucureşti Băneasa station rather than Bucureşti Nord. This is cheap but extremely comfortable. I chose a cabin with two large bunks made up with laundered sheets and a wash handbasin which doubled as a bedside table when covered. The train makes steady, comfortable progress, following the valley of the Siret, a tributary of the Danube, deep into the Carpathian foothills, and arrives at 0600. An earlier train leaves Bucureşti Nord at 2300 and arrives at Suceava and Suceava Nord soon after 0500.

Tourist Information Centre Str Nicolae Bălcescu 2 (tel 21297, 10944), hours 0800-2000.

Central Post Office Str N Bălcescu, hours 0800-2000.

Banking Hours 0900-1200.

Accommodation
Middle range
Hotel Bucovina, Str Ana Ipătescu 5 (tel 17048).
Hotel Suceava, Str N Bălcescu 2 (tel 22497).

Budget
Some private rooms are available.

Camping
Plentiful — contact tourist information.

Restaurants
Clasic, Str N Bălcescu, open 0900-2200.

Sightseeing
Reminiscent of Rila in Bulgaria, the area just west of Suceava contains many monasteries, most with churches painted inside and out in the 16th Century. The oldest and most famous is Voroneţ, dating from 1488; this is known as the 'Sistine Chapel of the East' because of its fine frescoes in an unusual shade of blue. At Humor, a village just to the north, the monastery has frescoes depicting the devil as a woman, at Suceviţa the monastery has a wealth of frescoes, from portraits of Plato to the 'Arabian Nights', and that at Moldoviţa also has fine frescoes, with a good little museum. Contact the Suceava tourist office for tour

Suceava Nord

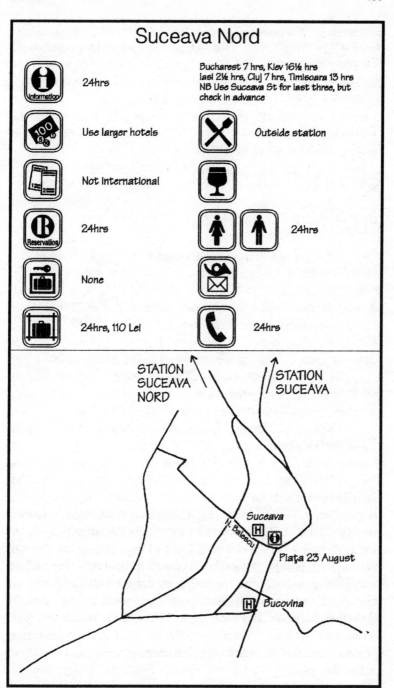

24hrs

Bucharest 7 hrs, Kiev 16½ hrs
Iasi 2½ hrs, Cluj 7 hrs, Timisoara 13 hrs
NB Use Suceava St for last three, but
check in advance

Use larger hotels

Outside station

Not International

24hrs

24hrs

None

24hrs, 110 Lei

24hrs

STATION SUCEAVA NORD

STATION SUCEAVA

Suceava

Piaţa 23 August

Bucovina

N. Balcecu

information; Voroneț and Humor can be reached by regular buses from Gura Humorului station, on the main line west from Suceava, Sucevița by bus from Rădăuți, north of Suceava, and Moldovița by a branch line north from Vama, west of Gura Humorului (get off at Vatra Moldoviței station).

In Suceava itself there are similar churches, with less interesting frescoes, and museums. Much of the city is new development, intended as a model for other towns. The wooded landscape is typical of Moldavia, with many hotels for those who enjoy mountain pursuits.

CLUJ

Cluj is well placed in the Romanian railway network and a good centre for the independent rail traveller. It is served by trains from Budapest to Tîrgu Mureş and Braşov, but through Budapest-Bucharest trains all now take the route to the south via Arad. There are also fast trains from Bucharest and on the cross-country axis from Suceava to Timişoara. The rail journey between Suceava and Cluj is a wonderful way of seeing the eastern Carpathians, passing through valleys of orchards sprinkled with small towns of red roofed houses and churches. It is desperately poor compared with western Europe, with old railway stock and an absence of platforms. The train sanitation is poor with no water or paper (although this is likely to be the case on almost all Romanian trains), while the buffet is basic; but the view compensates. On the way, the view of rural life indicates that time has stood still for more than half a century. Hay is collected in small amounts and stoves are still fueled with wood, collected largely by hand. The train passes through the attractive spa of Vatra Dornei and then winds through valleys with good views to the highest levels. There are plenty of branches for freight transport, especially the extraction of logs. Inside, as you view this scene, the restaurant serves a standard meal for less than $1 including beer. At Salva we have cleared the top and the route opens out into the wide valley of the Someş. Corn and sunflower predominate and the signs of population increase until we arrive at the city of Cluj.

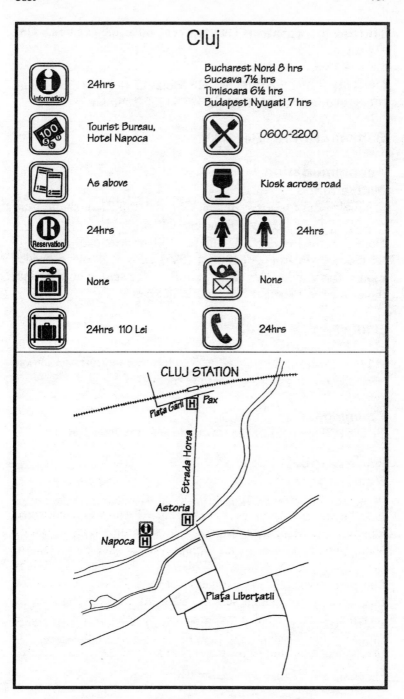

Cluj

24hrs

Bucharest Nord 8 hrs
Suceava 7½ hrs
Timisoara 6½ hrs
Budapest Nyugati 7 hrs

Tourist Bureau,
Hotel Napoca

0600-2200

As above

Kiosk across road

24hrs

24hrs

None

None

24hrs 110 Lei

24hrs

CLUJ STATION

Piața Garii — Pax

Strada Horea

Astoria

Napoca

Piața Libertatii

Tourist Information Centre in Hotel Napoca (tel 180 715)
see below.

Central Post Office Str Gh Doja 33 (tel 104135), hours
0700-2000 Monday to Friday, 0700-1300 Saturday.

Banking Hours 0800-1200.

Accommodation
Middle range
Hotel Napoca, Str Józsa Béla 3, Cluj (tel 180 715), single from
47,400 lei ($27.40), twin from 60,100 lei, 350 beds.
Hotel Astoria, Str Horea 3, Cluj (tel 130166), single from 26,100
lei ($16), twin from 40,300 lei ($25), also 3, 4 and 6 bedded
rooms. Basic, with TV; about 1km from the station heading into
the centre, on the right just before the river.

Budget
Hotel Pax, Piaţa Gării 1, Cluj (tel 132315), single from 20,000 lei
($13), twin from 39,300 lei ($25). Opposite the railway station;
very cheap and grotty, inspect the room first.

Camping
Feleacu, 7km south of the town, close to the river Racilor.

Sightseeing
The tourist office produces a guide which lists most items of
interest in the city. There is a fine Gothic cathedral on the central
Piaţa Unirii (formerly Libertăţii), the Transylvanian History
Museum on Piaţa Muzeului, the ethnographic museum at Str
Memorandumului 21, and a number of other interesting museums
and monuments.

Cluj is a convenient base for excursions within the north western
part of Romania. Try to get to the area of Maramureş, beyond the
town of Baia Mare or by the branch north from Salva to Sighet,
although the time conscious may find buses more convenient. The
wooden churches and houses are gorgeous, and folk customs are
more alive here than almost anywhere else in Europe.

The route from Cluj to Bucharest is amongst the most scenic in the country. More than half the journey is through Transylvania and the southern Carpathians, passing close to the Bucegi range at the former royal resort of Sinaia. Dracula country begins about three hours from Cluj with his birthplace of Sighişoara, still perhaps the most perfect medieval townscape in Europe. You can see it from almost any train from Cluj or Budapest, but it really is worth a stop. The only hotel is the Steaua on Str 1 Decembrie (single from 10,250 lei, twin from 18,200 lei), and there is a camp site on top of the hill behind the station.

Another 1¾ hours further towards Bucharest is the city of Braşov, guarding the entrance to the Carpathian passes; this was a stronghold of the Saxons, who came in the early 13th Century and built up their own very distinctive culture here, with fortified churches in many of the villages between Braşov, Sighişoara and Sibiu. The streets are largely lined with baroque buildings, but they are dominated by the 14th-15th Century Gothic Black Church and the 15th Century Town Hall, now a local history museum. The most expensive hotels are the Carpaţi (or Aro-Palas) at Bdul Eroilor 9 (tel 42840) and the Capitol (Bdul Eroilor 19, tel 18920); cheaper ones are the Parc (Str N Iorga 2, tel 19460), Postăvarul and Coroana (Str Republicii 62, tel 44330), and Aro-Sport (Str Iuliu Maniu 32, tel 19464), as well as a dozen others at Poiana Braşov, Romania's main ski resort 20 minutes away by bus 20. From bus station no 2, near the minor Bartolomei station, you can take a bus to the castle of Bran, which is sold to the coach parties as 'Dracula's castle', and looks as if it should be even though it has next to nothing to do with the historic Vlad Ţepeş (the Impaler).

An alternative route to Braşov or Bucharest is via Sibiu, the cultural capital of the Saxons, on a non-electrified line parallel to the main line through Sighişoara; the trains are slow, but again the city is well worth seeing for its Gothic Saxon churches and fortifications and its baroque streets and squares. The Împărator Romanilor, Bulevard and Continental hotels are expensive; cheaper alternatives are the Podul Minciunilor at Str Azilului 1 (tel 17259), a small private guesthouse, the motel and camp site to the south in the Pădurea Dumbrava (trolleybus 1 from the

station, tel 22920), or private rooms from the agency at Str
Bălcescu 1.

TIMIŞOARA

Timişoara, a city of around 300,000, entered the news in 1989
when it triggered the downfall of the Ceauşescu dictatorship.
Demonstrations against the internal exile of Pastor Lászlo Tokes
resulted in many deaths, and bullet damage is visible on the walls
of many buildings. This historic city is an important economic,
scientific and cultural centre, with a population of Germans,
Hungarians, Serbs, Slovaks and Romanians. As the leading city
of the Banat, Romania's western fringe, it shows the architectural
imprints of two centuries of Hapsburg rule.

Direct trains run from Bucharest via the Iron Gates of the
Danube, but you are more likely to approach via Arad, an hour
to the north, the main gateway to Romania from the west. Arad
is not a place in which to linger: in fact 'arid' would be a more
appropriate name. In summer the fly-ridden waiting room renders
the station useful only for leaving bags. There is little to see here
close to the station, although the town centre has many
monumental turn-of-the-century buildings. Timişoara is a
complete contrast. At Timişoara Nord, the main station, turn left
out of the station on Bulevardul Republicii and you are soon in
the city centre.

Tourist Information Centre Bdul Republicii 6 (tel 36532).

Central Post Office Bdul Revoluţie 1989 2 (tel 11050),
hours 0630-2020 Monday to Friday, 0830-1400 Saturday.

Banking Hours 0800-1200.

Accommodation
Upper range
Hotel Continental, Bdul Revoluţie 3 (tel 34144), single from
52,000 lei ($52), twin from 66,500 lei. Central location near the
Civic Park; American bar and nightclub.

Timişoara Nord

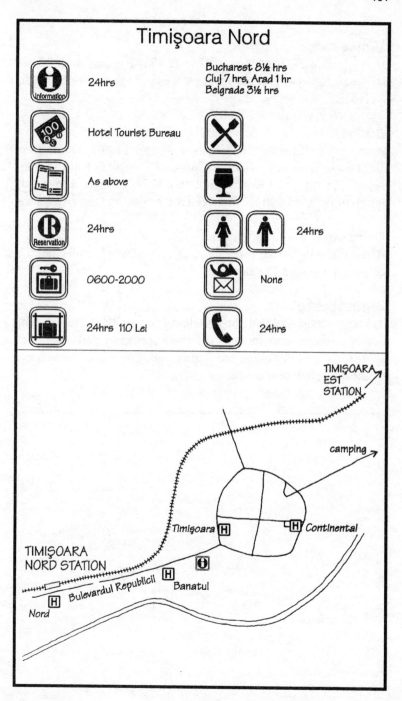

24hrs

Bucharest 8½ hrs
Cluj 7 hrs, Arad 1 hr
Belgrade 3½ hrs

Hotel Tourist Bureau

As above

24hrs

0600-2000   None

24hrs 110 Lei   24hrs

TIMIŞOARA
EST
STATION

camping

Timişoara [H]   [H] Continental

TIMIŞOARA
NORD STATION

Bulevardul Republicii   Banatul

[H]
Nord

Middle range
Hotel Timişoara, Str Mărăşeşti 1 (tel 37714), rooms from 27,800
lei single and twin. Close to the station, at the city end of Bdul
Republicii.

Budget
Hotel Nord, Bdul Gen I Dragalina 47 (tel 12308), single from
10,500 lei, twin from 20,600. Opposite Timişoara Nord station.
Hotel Banatul, Bdul Republicii 5 (tel 37772), single from 9,000
lei, twin from 15,000 lei. Between the station and the city centre.

Camping
Aleea Pădurea Verde, just east of the city; tram 1, trolleybus 11,
or near Timişoara Est station.

Sightseeing
The city centre is ideal for a walking tour with streets opening
out into squares and gardens. It is well served by parks and open
spaces, particularly along the Bega canal. There is a good choice
of theatre, cinema and opera.

Romanian Railways

by Tim Burford

The CFR (Romanian Railways) used to have an excellent reputation, before being overwhelmed by the fuel shortages and economic collapse of the late Ceauşescu period. Now the passenger trains are less overcrowded but remain the main means of long distance travel. You can either pay a standard fare to travel in slow all-stops trains (*cursă* or *personal/persoane*), or pay a small supplement for faster (*expres, rapid* or *accelerat*) trains, which will often carry couchette or sleeping cars on overnight services. *Expres* (usually international) and *rapid* trains are all-reserved, while for *accelerats*, the main inter-urban services, you will normally be given a reservation, except from less important stations which do not have a quota of seats and will just sell you an unreserved ticket. Most towns have an *Agenţia de Voiaj CFR* in the centre (usually closed at weekends) where you can buy tickets in advance.

Most compartments are non-smoking (*nefumatori*), with lines of men (mostly) smoking in the corridors, but this doesn't usually apply in the open double-deck and narrow gauge coaches. There will usually be very poor lighting and no water or paper in the toilets; on-train catering is very rare. To travel in real comfort you may choose to pay for first class or only use the international services from Hungary and the west via Cluj, Sighişoara, Braşov and Sinaia, which have better quality stock, mainly Hungarian or Austrian.

Timetables are listed on two boards, headed *sosire* (arrival) and *plecare* (departure), giving the train type and its number, its destination, its track (counted outwards from the main station building), and sometimes the duration of its stop. Trains run not at regular intervals throughout the day, as in the west, but on a fairly ad-hoc basis; only on the Bucharest-Constanţa line is there anything approaching a regular hourly service, but even this falls apart in the opposite direction. Between Bucharest and Ploieşti (and perhaps Braşov) there could be an hourly service along the lines of western InterCity services, but this is complicated by the many international services on this route. In common with most European railways CFR operates a seven-day timetable with engineering work carried out throughout the week (less being needed than in Britain due to the lower speeds). Most main lines are signalled for reversible working, but there is also a considerable margin for delay built into the timetable; for a naturally unpunctual nation trains tend to run remarkably punctually.

Under the Comecon pooling system electric locomotives were built for the eastern bloc by Skoda in Czechoslovakia, trams were built by Tatra, also in Czechoslovakia, buses by Ikarus in Hungary, double-deck coaches by VEB Waggonbau in East Germany, and diesel locomotives in Romania. At the same time most of the countries of the Soviet bloc also built equipment for themselves, and Romania had a swop arrangement with Yugoslavia, whereby six-axled electric locomotives built by Electroputere under license from ASEA of Sweden were exchanged for the four-axled version built by Rade Koncar in Zagreb. In all 885 of these 5100kW Class 40 machines were built for CFR from 1967, as well as 103 for Yugoslavia and 45 for Bulgaria; there is also a larger version known as class 60.

Main-line diesels are 1550kW machines built by Electroputere, Craiova, to a Brown-Boveri design (also exported to Poland, Bulgaria and China), and the 23 August works in Bucharest have also produced a range of smaller locomotives, from 1000kW to 1700kW, under licence from Alco. Diesel railcars were introduced before the Second World War both for branch services and for *accelerats* in the style of the *Flying Hamburger*; they still survive on local services around Arad, Sibiu and Rîmnicu Vîlcea. Steam traction is virtually extinct on the standard-gauge network, although many steam locomotives can be seen dumped in sidings near major cities. These were mainly of type 050 (meaning an 0-10-0 wheel arrangement), as well as types 150 and 230.

The Bucharest Metro is 59.8km long with 39 stations (at an average spacing of 1.53km), all underground apart from the depots, at the standard gauge of 1432mm; it is unusual as almost the only metro in eastern Europe not built as a clone of the Moscow metro. Line 1 (marked in yellow) was the first to open in 1978 and now stretches 30.7km from Republica west to Industrilor and Gara de Nord; the north-south line 2 (marked in blue) opened in 1986-87, and now stretches 19.2km from Pipera to IMGB, and the orbital line 3 (marked in red) opened in 1989, stretching 9.9km from the Garaă de Nord to Dristor 2 (interchange with line 1). In practice line 3 trains generally continue from Gara de Nord to Republica over line 1.

There are plans for this system to be doubled in the next decade, although it is likely to take considerably longer than this. The first two sections are to be line 7, a 4.8km branch of line 1 from Nicolae Grigorescu east to Linia de Centura, and line 4, 6.4km north from the Garǎ de Nord to Laromet. There are also plans for line 5, 16km from Pantelimon to Drumul Taberei via Eroilor, and line 6, 17km southwest from Colentina to Rahova.

The Metro operates from 0500 to 2300, at intervals of 10-12 minutes maximum; in mid 1993 the fare was L50, fed into a slot on the entrance turnstiles (you can always get change from a booth nearby). Stations are slightly better lit than they once were, but the interchanges in particular can be confusing, with poor signposting and station names hidden by the trains themselves.

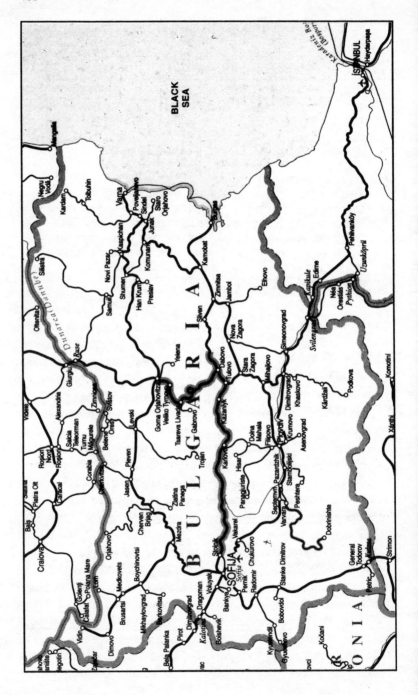

Chapter 8

Bulgaria

Area: 110,910 km² (42,823 sq miles) Population: 9 million
Capital: Sofia Population: 1,120,000

Bulgaria is the southernmost eastern European state covered here.
For close on half a century, rule by the Bulgarian Communist
Party discouraged independent travel and most visitors have
tended to come in parties to the Black Sea coast resorts.
Relaxation of movement following the 1989 changes now mean
that, provided you have a visa, you can travel virtually anywhere
and discover the rich history of this country.

The Bulgarians are extremely proud of their past and it is they
who are responsible for the large number of archaeological sites
which are visible today. For example, in Plovdiv, Roman remains
are visible underneath a contemporary square, and a road tunnel
has been constructed under the amphitheatre rather than destroy
it. Unlike neighbouring Romania, good examples of every period
of architecture may be seen from Roman times to the mosques of
the Byzantine Empire and beyond. Today's town halls are former
Communist Party headquarters, 'given' to the people.

Since the Second World War, Bulgaria was one of the most
loyal members of the Soviet Bloc. Economic activity was in the
hands of the Communist Party and former head of state Todor
Zhivkov. With his resignation in November 1989, after 35 years
as leader, private enterprise has begun to develop slowly.
However, after such a long period of isolation from the West, few
Bulgarians know exactly how to go about operating private

business. Of those who are learning fast, the most prominent you will meet are money changers and room vendors. Be on your guard against the former as you may receive a poor rate or worthless notes.

Generally, the people of Bulgaria are generous and hospitable. They welcome the opportunity to meet Western travellers and will often invite you to stay with them. It is traditional for Bulgarians to put their home first and you will be surprised at how comfortable their homes are. You should remember that, currently, it is difficult for them to visit Western countries without an invitation (which means staying with someone) so do keep that in mind before accepting too much hospitality yourself.

One way of preparing for independent travel here is to learn the Cyrillic alphabet. Although some signs and symbols will be understandable, the bulk of notices, street names, etc, are not. Familiarity with a few simple phrases is also well worth the effort.

GEOGRAPHY
Bulgaria is a little under half the size of the United Kingdom. The River Danube forms a natural frontier with Romania to the north. There are plains on the southern side of the river where much of Bulgaria's food is grown. The Balkan mountains then form an east west barrier in the middle of the country stretching from former Yugoslavia through to the Black Sea. Most of the western half of the country is mountainous and similar terrain forms the southern border with Greece. Some lower-lying ground is found stretching from Plovdiv east to Burgas. With more than one third of the country mountainous, it is not surprising that population is sparse or that rail travel is slow. However, the beauty of the landscape and tremendous diversity make Bulgaria a most attractive destination to see by rail.

CURRENCY
1 lev = 100 stotinki. Currently, the lev (plural leva) is not freely changeable and cannot be purchased in the UK. The official rate against hard currencies continues to be very good value for Western visitors as the cost of living continues to be very low.

SOFIA
Sofia Central Station
This is a modern white marble station on three levels. It is also the most international of Bulgarian stations with a liberal use of pictograms and translation of most Cyrillic signs. Platforms tend to use Roman numerals and the train could be at either side. So, for example, **II** will mean either side of platform 2. Double check if uncertain.

Tourist Information Centre, Knjaz Dondukov 37 (tel 88 44 30), open 0700-2200. Central, 5 minutes from Sheraton Sofia Hotel (see below).

Banking Hours Monday to Friday 0800-1200, 1300-1700.

Accommodation
None is immediately apparent in the station square, although the accommodation agency will help with private rooms. Sofia Central is, in fact, quite close to the centre where a larger choice of hotels is available.

Upper range
Sheraton Sofia Hotel, Balkan, 2 Lenin Square, Sofia (tel 87 65 41), single $85, twin $126.

This large, luxurious, very central, 600-room American style international hotel has a 24-hour restaurant. Fish and chips were available for the equivalent of £9.

Middle range
Novotel Europa, 131 Georgi Dimitrov, 1000 Sofia (tel 31261), twin rooms from around $90. The top of the hotel block can be seen from the station to the front left as you face the square. Air conditioned, a group tourist hotel, good English spoken and money exchanged.
Grand Hotel Sofia, Narodno Subranic Square, 1000 Sofia (tel 87 88 21). Twin room from around $80. More central than the Novotel, with very friendly, helpful staff; $13 buys a great meal with wine.

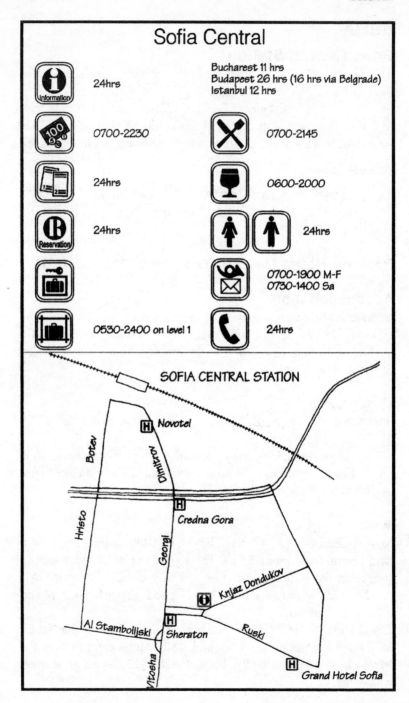

Budget

Xotel Cpedha Copa (Sredna Gora), Place Lavov Most, Sofia (tel 83 53 11), single from $12, twin $20. Very basic accommodation with a wash hand basin, little English, no facilities. The *Lavov Most* (Lion Bridge), which the hotel overlooks, is a good landmark and lies between the station and the city centre. It is around 15 minutes walk from either.

Private rooms

These range from 70 leva (35 leva per bed) — $10 for 2 star up to 80-90 leva — $12 for 3 star. Try to check out your location first but many are close to the station or centre. At these prices it is hardly worth looking for a hostel or camp site and the locals benefit directly. Check these out in the station accommodation office or speak to a local. A street plan is helpful here and is available in the station.

City Transport and Orientation

Although Sofia is a small capital city, you will find a street plan useful, especially if you can read the Cyrillic script. It is possible to obtain one in advance from the Bulgarian National Tourist Office in London, 18 Princes Street, W1R 7RE. This will help you walk easily around the central areas without public transport.

Contrary to the opinion of some other writers, Sofia does warrant a few days stay. It dates back over 3,000 years and, although it suffered considerable damage during the last war, there is still plenty to see. The best way to get a feel of the city, if you have time, is on foot in the streets.

If you do decide to use public transport, you have a choice of bus, trolleybus or tram. Your street plan will assist you with the route numbers and the services stretch into the suburbs. There is a flat fare and, as official guidance says 'tickets are bought beforehand and perforated inside the vehicle'. A carnet of 10 tickets can also be bought; obtain your tickets from kiosks or from the driver. Tram and trolleybus lines operate from 0400 to 0100 with buses operating until midnight.

Taxis are plentiful and available at stands all over the city. Dial 142 to make an advance booking.

Restaurants and Eating Out

Do not judge the food by the quality purveyed in the restaurant at Sofia Central station. It is not typical; in fact, had I not tasted a range of dishes, I would have thought it unbelievable. The surroundings are also dirty. Only if you are really hungry will you appreciate greasy, watery soup accompanied by sausages, salad and bread.

Prices in Sofia are low so you have plenty of choice in most price ranges. There is a wide choice of restaurants on Vitosha, south of the Sheraton. This leads up to the National Palace of Culture, which also has a good restaurant. Many local restaurants are to be found at the basement of buildings and are marked *PECTOPAHT* (this means restaurant and is pronounced the same). Bulgarian food uses locally grown ingredients, and a typical meal will include pork, yoghurt, tomatoes, rice, fetta style cheese, cucumber and herbs. The home produced wine is delicious. Try, for example, Trakia, a smooth, fruity red, or Melnik, a red with more tannin.

All the larger hotels have restaurants serving a range of dishes. Staff speak English and are happy to recommend something to suit your palate. Here you will be able to order a beef steak with garnish at an unbelievably cheap price. At the Grand Hotel Sofia $13 will buy you steak flambéd in liqueur, vegetables, salad, a bottle of wine, coffee and brandy, all served in an opulent dining room with a band singing in English. On many very cheap menus it is hard to avoid a staple diet of pork steak and sliced tomato so head for the better hotels, if you have a delicate stomach or seek variety.

Imported beers and drinks are available but much more expensive. Try to insist on local products wherever possible as they are usually fine. There are many takeaways to choose from. Pizzas and chicken are readily available but you might also try their puff pastries filled with cheese (banitsa).

A final word. Do not always expect a written menu. Waiting staff tend to offer a verbal version as dishes change, printing is expensive and prices fluctuate (mainly upwards).

Sofia Excursions
The Centre

Tram numbers 1, 7 and 15 run from Sofia Central to the National Palace of Culture and beyond. This is essentially north-south through the centre of the city. As indicated earlier, a walking tour is the best way. From the station, along Georgi Dimitrov, past the Novotel, you come to Lavov Most, the unmistakable Lion Bridge. Head south from here and you will be amazed at the architectural diversity, both religious and secular. The Bania Bashi Mosque is unavoidable as it stands in the centre of the street.

There are more than 250 historic monuments. Especially recommended are St George Rotunda, the Church of St Sophia, of St Petka Samardjiiska, the Boyana Church and the Alexander Nevski Memorial Church and the Mausoleum (now empty) of Georgi Dimitrov, the working class militant and first leader of the People's Republic of Bulgaria who died in Moscow in 1949. The National History Museum, currently under partial restoration, resembles a palace and you will not be disappointed with its contents. You could also include visits to the National Archaelogical Museum, the National Ethnographic Museum, the National Gallery of Art, the Natural History Museum and the National Military Museum. Art interests are also served by the Foreign Art Gallery, the Sofia Art Gallery and the Central Art Gallery. The National Palace of Culture hosts performances, festivals and exhibitions as well as being a good example of modern architecture.

However, what will really give you the flavour of the city is to walk down some of the narrow streets as well. You will then begin to become familiar with Bulgarian city life and discover aspects which guidebooks can overlook.

Day Visits
Mount Vitosha

Mount Vitosha, surrounded by a national park, lies 5 miles southwest of Sofia. The Information Office of Balkantourist can advise on excursions or travel here by bus, tram and cable car.

Rila Monastery (Rilski Monastir)

This is the largest monastery in Bulgaria, high up in the Rila
mountain range some 55km south of Sofia. It is possible to reach
it by public transport and the journey is very interesting as you
are in the company of locals. But, if you choose to travel this
way, allow more than one day. Train to Kocerinovo (on Athens
route after Stanke Dimitrov 2 hours) then about 1 hour on an
antique bus through Rila and Pastra. If time is short, take a
Balkantourist coach tour.

PLOVDIV

Plovdiv is the second city of Bulgaria with around 350,000
inhabitants. It is one of the most ancient cities in Europe and
possibly the most important from an archaeological viewpoint in
the Balkan peninsular.

The amphitheatre dates from the 2nd Century AD. With their
usual fastidiousness for preservation, the Bulgarians have build a
road tunnel (Georgi Dimitrov St) underneath it. In addition there
are Byzantine fortress walls and many fine houses from the
National Revival period of the mid-nineteenth century.

The city has not always been known as Plovdiv. It was
originally called Eumolpia, then Philippopolis after Philip II of
Macedon and, in Roman times, Trimontium after the three hills
on which it was then built. Other names have included Upper
Flavia, Pulpudeva and Puldin. It has been called Plovdiv since
1636.

Plovdiv is not just for lovers of heritage, it has an international
flavour with good entertainment and restaurant facilities. It is host
to international fairs and the International Chamber Music
Festival. It is also a centre for Bulgarian artists and crafts people.

Accommodation
Upper range
Novotel, Plovdiv, 2 Zlatyu Boyadjiev St, 4000 Plovdiv (tel 5 58
92), single from $60, twin $100.

Furthest away from the station on the bank of the Maritsa river
opposite the old city, the hotel is quite new. The five star

Plovdiv

24hrs Bulgarian/
Russian

Sofia 2½ hrs
Varna 7 hrs   Burgas 7 hrs
Gorna Orjahovitza 5½ hrs

See banks or hotels

1100-2230

Rila Bureau near
Bulgaria Hotel
0800-1900 M-F

1100-2230

24hrs

24hrs
No showers

0800-1900 M-F

24hrs (but 2 x ½ hr
breaks - check notice)

24hrs

Novotel [H]

R. Maritsa

Old
Plovdiv

Ruski

Lilyana Dimitrova

Sašo   Dimitrov

Leipzig

[H]

Vasil Aprilov

Boulevard

Ivan Vazov

[H][i]
Trimontium

[i]
PLOVDIV CENTRAL STATION

accommodation includes swimming pools, solarium, tennis courts, saunas, nightclubs and restaurants.

Middle range
Hotel Trimontium, Kapitan Raicho Str, Plovdiv 4000 (tel 2 34 91) single from $41, twin $60-64.

Very central location. 10 minutes walk from the station along Ivan Vazov, surrounded by both the old and new city; money exchange, information and a friendly staff.

Budget
Hotel Leipzig, 76 Boulevard Ruski, 4000 Plovdiv (tel 23 22 01), single from $22, twin $28, including breakfast; nearest to the station, basic but comfortable rooms.

Private rooms
These are becoming ever more popular. Some residents will offer you a room at the station, otherwise the tourist information service at the Trimontium or the one which may open at the station should be consulted. Expect to pay between $8 to $15.

Camping
Sites are some distance from Plovdiv station. The nearest is Motel/camping Deveti-Kilometre, 9km to the west of Plovdiv on the route E80 to Sofia by the river Maritsa. There are bungalows here, as well, and a swimming pool.

Sightseeing
The City
Many of the sights are within easy walking distance. The mix of old and new is comparable with Athens except that the Bulgarians really treasure their ancient environment.

There are many nooks and crannies to explore and the old city is a good place to start. Above Georgi Dimitrov tunnel, you will see the amphitheatre and beyond, contained within the old walls of the city, there are numerous monuments and restaurants. There are other steep hills which give good views of the city, each offering a different vantage point and sometimes a surprise at their summit.

It is within the old city that you will come across the famous art and craft wares of the community, good for viewing or buying. Below the walls, at the south, near Nikola Ginev is a fruit and vegetable market where, in the summer season, you can buy fresh grapes and figs from local traders.

Bachovo Monastery
A Balkantourist coach tour will take you here some 30km south east of the city. It is Bulgaria's second largest monastery after Rila (*see Sofia section*) and was built in 1083.

Pamporovo
One of Bulgaria's most famous skiing resorts is 85km south of Plovdiv. On the road from Bachovo, you travel through the Rhodope mountains giving you fine views of the spectacular scenery of southern Bulgaria.

The Valley of the Roses
Plovdiv is surrounded by fields of roses. Around 70% of the rose oil used by the world's leading cosmetic manufacturers comes from this region. If you are visiting in the first week of June, go to Kazenluk and Karlovo, north of Plovdiv, for the Festival of the Rose. At other times, such a large number of rose fields is a very impressive sight.

VELIKO TURNOVO

This former capital of Bulgaria is a quite outstanding settlement. It lies in and around the gorge valley of the River Jantra, 5 hours north east of Plovdiv on the line to the border city of Ruse (3 hours). Whether you approach this old city from the north or the south, you will be impressed with the scenery of this natural pass through the Balkans. From Gorna Orjahovitza, heading south towards Veliko Turnovo, look out on your right for what is reputed to be the largest automated freight terminal in Eastern Europe. Later, you get an excellent view of the old city of Veliko Turnovo as you travel towards it on the right. The buildings cling to the valley with the river flowing below.

Understandably, Veliko Turnovo is very attractive for tourists but there is little room for new building. Accommodation is, therefore, at a premium and can be expensive compared with surrounding areas. Although you may wish to experience a night here, it can also be worth staying in some less popular places nearby (contact Tourist Information).

Accommodation
Upper range
Interhotel Veliko Turnovo, Emilia Popova 2, 5000 Veliko Turnovo, (tel 3 05 71), single from $50, twin $82, including breakfast. Modern luxury four star hotel which includes a tourist service office; 200 rooms, two restaurants, fitness centre including swimming pool and shops.

Budget
Hotel Etur, 1 Ivailo St. Veliko Turnovo, (tel 2 68 61), single from $10, twin $20.

Camping
Sveta Gora Motel and Campsite, left out of railway station and first right, 1km at end of road.

Sightseeing
Collect one of Balkantourist's excellent maps. This is useful for walking tours around the rabbit warren of streets and will save you time (available from Interhotel Veliko Turnovo). Bus numbers 12 or 13 moving right from the station will take you to the end of Marmarlijska near to the centre. The equivalent walk takes about 30 minutes.

You will need at least a full day to begin to appreciate the delights of Veliko Turnovo. The old city is situated on three hills Tsarevets, Trapezitsa and Sveta Gora. These are to the east of today's centre where the Jantra river loops around them. Tsarevets Hill reveals fortress walls, gates and battle towers. Trapezitsa contains many churches, preserved and restored as medieval foundations as well as remains of fortifications. Sveta

Veliko Turnovo

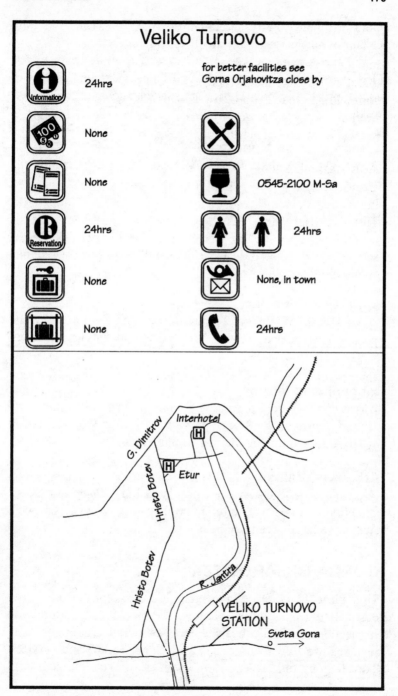

for better facilities see
Gorna Orjahovitza close by

Information — 24hrs

100 — None

— None

Reservation — 24hrs

— None

— None

— (restaurant)

— 0545-2100 M-Sa

— 24hrs

— None, in town

— 24hrs

Gora was particularly important between the 12th and 14th Centuries and is today the site of the university.

The area around the Georgi Dimitrov Blagoev is worth a visit. Here you will find many craft workshops, cafes and aspects of contemporary city life. Other sights listed below are within easy reach.

Transfiguration Monastery
(7km west of Veliko Turnovo) founded in 14th Century and rebuilt during the 19th Century; murals, icons, library.

Holy Trinity Monastery
(7km north of Veliko Turnovo) was founded in 1070 and became a major literary centre in the 14th Century. The monastery and church was built in 1847.

Kilifarevo Monastery
(17km south of Veliko Turnovo) was founded in 1350 and became a literary centre for monks including those of neighbouring countries.

Nicopolis ad Istrum
(18km north of Veliko Turnovo) Ruins of the administrative and military centre of the Roman province of Lower Moesia founded in 106AD by Emperor Marcus Ulpius Trajanus.

Arbanassi Village
(4km northeast) A very well preserved old village and tourist attraction. Museum exhibition well worth a visit as well. Accommodation available here.

GORNA ORJAHOVITZA

This place is more of a communications centre than a tour destination from Veliko Turnovo. Gorna has an airport with connections to Sofia. It also serves as a 'rail crossroads' with regular Ruse-Plovdiv trains and Ruse-Sofia, Sofia-Varna services. Travellers by rail can therefore use it as an overnight stop from

Gorna Orjahovitza

Information 24hrs			Berlin Lichtenberg 4 hrs Leipzig 1½ hrs Eisenach 1 hr
None – use Balkantourist or hotels			0900-2300 (closed 1400-1600)
24hrs			24hrs
Reservation 24hrs			24hrs
None			0700-2100 M-F 0800-1400 Sa-Su
24hrs			24hrs

many parts of the country. It is Bulgaria's second largest railway centre after Sofia.

Another advantage in stopping here is that the prices are far lower than popular tourist destinations. The town lives in the present and you will see contemporary Bulgarian life in the market and in the bars, restaurants and shops. Linger a while in the main square, Georgi Izmirliev, where the former Communist Party building is now the Town Hall.

There is no street plan for Gorna Orjahovitza as there is little specifically for tourists. Head for Georgi Izmirliev Square if you plan to stay a while and consult the very helpful Balkantourist staff. In the square itself, you will find the Rahovice Hotel, from 100 leva in 1991 (£4 for three star equivalent). The Racchovetz (Paxobell) is even cheaper. However, with the political changes and privatisation, expect more choice and higher prices.

THE BLACK SEA COAST

Bulgaria is blessed with a very varied 378km coastline along the Black Sea. There are vast sandy beaches, beautiful bays, cliffs, wooded hills, vineyards and gardens. You will find the sea especially inviting after a long rail journey. The salinity is much lower than the Mediterranean and the water is generally shallow and clean. The reliable sunshine and the favourable climate in the summer make a visit hard to resist.

It is not just the geographical features of the coastline which are varied. The Bulgarian government has concentrated on capturing some of the package tour market of both eastern and western Europe. Demand has been impressive and to cater for groups, several modern seaside resorts have been developed. These resorts provide everything for their customers and therefore entertainment in the cities of Bourgas and Varna is less comprehensive than might be expected.

Those who prefer the atmosphere of small fishing villages might choose to go south of Bourgas where there is less development. Sunny Beach to the north of Bourgas is Bulgaria's largest seaside resort. The Sunny Beach nightclub and casino is also the largest on the coast.

From Varna, it should be possible to access most of the coast except the very south. Within a day's travel are many modern seaside resorts, historical sites and buildings, quiet beaches, fishing villages and inland villages.

Varna and Bourgas are the two main railway termini. Varna is the larger of the two and Bourgas lies about two hours south. Carriages are very crowded in the summer months to both destinations. There are direct international links at this time from such cities as Warsaw and Prague. If you decide to go, you will be sure of an unrivalled international mix of travel companions from eastern and western Europe.

Varna
Accommodation
Upper range
Grand Hotel Varna, 9006 Drouzhba Resort, Bulgaria (tel 86 14

Varna

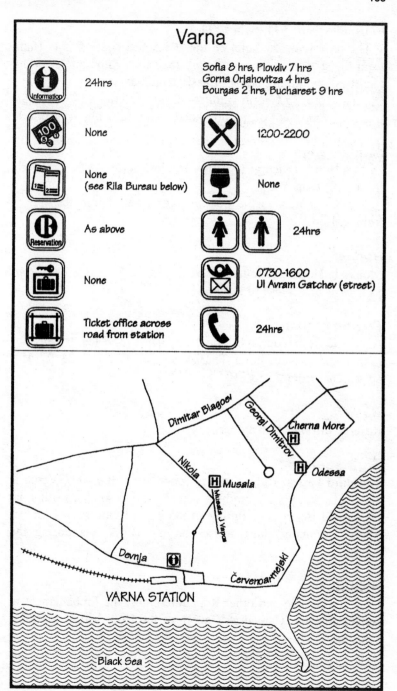

Information — 24hrs

Sofia 8 hrs, Plovdiv 7 hrs
Gorna Orjahovitza 4 hrs
Bourgas 2 hrs, Bucharest 9 hrs

None

1200-2200

None
(see Rila Bureau below)

None

Reservation — As above

24hrs

None

0730-1600
Ul Avram Gatchev (street)

Ticket office across
road from station

24hrs

Dimitar Blagoev

Georgi Dimitrov

Cherna More

Nikola

Odessa

Musala

Musala J Varpa

Devnja

Červenoarmiejski

VARNA STATION

Black Sea

91) single from $95, twin $122.

The only five star hotel on the Black Sea coast, this is 10km from the station on the coast. Very luxurious with many sporting facilities, swimming pools, squash, tennis courts.

Cherno More, 35 Georgi Dimitrov Boulevard (tel 22 33 91). It is like the Grand, part of the Interhotel chain but with 3 star prices.

Middle range
Odessa Hotel, 1 Georgi Dimitrov Boulevard (tel 22 53 12) single from $20, twin $30.

A 2-3 star next to the Central Beach, and 5 minutes by taxi from station.

Budget
Moussala Hotel, 3 Moussala Street, (tel 22 39 35), single from $14, twin $24; close to station.

Private rooms
Available from Tourist Information Office for a fee; try also for rooms and private hotel Tourist Service OK (tel 23 07 10), apartments from $5 to $10.

Camping
Reserve through Balkantourist.

Sightseeing
The third largest Bulgarian city (population 300,000), Varna is also its largest port. From here you can sail to southern Bulgaria, Obsor and Bourgas or further to the port of Odessa in Ukraine. There are many short cruises on the Black Sea during the summer.

Historical
Roman Thermae and other Roman remains, the Embankment in Asparouti Park, Cathedral, Church of the Holy Virgin, National Theatre.

Museums
History and Art, Naval, Revolutionary Movement, National
Revival, Ethnographic, Natural Science, Man and Health, Georgi
Velcher Museum House and the Vladislav Varnenchik Museum
Park of Combat Friendship.

Other attractions
Aquarium, Copernicus Astronomy Complex, Zoo, Varna Art
Gallery and the Dolphinarium.

Resorts
Golden Sands 17km northeast on bus route 9 is a large resort.
Drouzhba, 10km northeast is on route 8. Kamchia, 30km south
has a vast beach and forest. These places with their hotel blocks
tend to isolate the tourist which is fine for some but one who
expected more action was overheard saying, 'Should have gone
to Malta'.

Bourgas
Sofia 6 hours, Plovdiv 4 hours, Varna 2 hours.

(Population 180,000), this is the rail gateway to the Black Sea
coast. You will arrive at the station in Bourgas Bay; there is an
information point. Tourist services are also available across the
road (Ivan Vasov) and 2 Parvi Mai St (47275).

Accommodation
Middle range
Hotel Bulgaria, Pǎrvi Maj, Bourgas (tel 4 28 20), single from
$25, twin $40. Close to the station, three restaurants, a nightclub
and currency exchange.

Budget
Primorets Hotel, Liljana Dimitrova (tel 4 41 17); 2-star. Turn
right or eastward from station; the hotel is situated at the bend in
Liljana Dimitrova close to the coasts.

Private Rooms
Available through tourist information.

Sightseeing
Historical
This is disappointing but not surprising given that Bourgas was no more than a village until the construction of the railway from Plovdiv.

Museums
Ethnographical and archaeological museums and an art gallery.

Entertainment
Several cinemas, two theatres, an opera and ballet.

Thirty-three kilometres north is the largest Bulgarian seaside resort, Sunny Beach, a Black Sea Blackpool.

The Bulgarian Railways

By Tim Burford

Bulgaria has always seen a great deal of transit traffic, mostly to Turkey, but with the virtual closure of former Yugoslavia much of the traffic to Greece is also passing through the country. Although 957km of new lines were built between 1944 and 1975, and the "Inner Ring" between Sofia, Mezdfra, Gorna Orjahovitza, Karlovo and Sofia was electrified from 1961, followed by "Outer Ring" to the ports of Varna and Bourgas, as well as to the Romanian border at Ruse and the Turkish border at Svilengrad, this was mainly intended for internal traffic across the country's steep mountain passes and for traffic from the then Soviet Union across Romania. Now 80% of traffic is electrically-hauled (with a quarter of it on the Sofia-Varna line). The emphasis is now on speeding transit traffic to Turkey and Greece, with electrification and upgrading of the main lines to the Greek border at Kulata and the Turkish border at Svilengrad (the latter for 160km/h running, 30km/h above the current maximum), as well as to the Serbian border at Dimitrovgrad.

Bulgaria has no native locomotive-building industry, so that BDZ's diesel locomotives originate in the Soviet Union, Romania, East Germany and Austria, with shunters from East Germany and Hungary, and narrow-gauge diesels from West Germany. Electric locomotives are from Skoda in Czechoslovakia and from Romania, and emus from the Riga works in Latvia.

The most interesting narrow-gauge line in Bulgaria is that from Septemvri (on the Sofia-Plovdiv line) to Velingrad, Bansko (an attractive ski resort in the Pirin range) and Dobrinishte. Sofia's metro is due to open late in 1994 (nine years late) as a 7.7km line from Ljubin (in the northwest) to the centre, with a later continuation southeast to Iskr.

Appendices

USEFUL ADDRESSES

Tourist offices in London
Bulgarian National Tourist Office
18 Princess Street
London W1R 7RE
Tel 071 499 6988

Czech and Slovak Republics (separate official National
Tourist Offices to open)
Čedok
49 Southwark Street
London SE1 1RU
Tel 071 378 6009

German National Tourist Office
Nightingale House
65 Curzon Street
London W1Y 7PE
Tel 071 495 3990

Hungary
Danube Travel Agency Ltd
6 Conduit Street
London W1R 9TG
Tel 071 493 0263

Poland
Polorbis
82 Mortimer Street
London W1N 7DE
Tel 071 636 2217

Romania
Romanian National Tourist Office (Carpati)
83A Marylebone High Street
London W1M 3DE
Tel 071 224 3692

(When requesting information by post, the offices appreciate an
A4 SAE enclosure, for reply.)

Embassies in London
Bulgaria
Embassy of the Republic of Bulgaria, Consular Section
188 Queen's Gate
London SW7 5HL
Tel 071 584 9400/9433
Open 0930-1230 Monday to Friday

Czech Republic
Embassy of the Czech Republic
28 Kensington Palace Gardens
London W8 4QY
Tel 071 727 4918

Germany
Embassy of the Federal Republic of Germany, Consular Section
23 Belgrave Square
London SW1X 8PZ
Tel 071 235 0165

Hungary
Embassy of the Republic of Hungary, Consular Department
35B Eaton Place
London SW1X 8BY
Tel 071 235 2664
Open 1000-1230 Monday to Friday

Poland

Consulate General of the Republic of Poland
73 New Cavendish Street
London W1N 7RB
Tel 071 580 0476
Open 1000-1400 Monday, Tuesday, Thursday, Friday, 1000-1200
Wednesday

Romania

Embassy of Romania, Consular Section
4 Palace Green
London W8 4QD
Tel 071 937 9667
Open 1000-1200 Monday to Friday

Slovak Republic

Embassy of the Slovak Republic, Visa Section
25 Kensington Palace Gardens
London W8 4QY
Tel 071 229 1255
Open 1000-1230 Monday to Friday

SELECTED LIST OF GUIDEBOOKS

Hiking Guide to Poland and Ukraine by Tim Burford (Bradt 1994)

The Rough Guide to Hungary by Dan Richardson (Rough Guides, 1993, 2nd edition)

The Rough Guide to Bulgaria by Jonathan Bonsfield and Dan Richardson (Rough Guides 1993)

The Rough Guide to Romania by Dan Richardson and Tim Burford (Rough Guides 1993)

Eastern Europe on a Shoestring by David Stanley (Lonely Planet 1991, 2nd edition)

Eastern Europe — A Travellers Companion by Phyllis Méras (Houghton Mifflin 1991)

Guide to Central Europe by Richard Basset (Viking 1987)

Guide to Czechoslovakia by Simon Hayman (Bradt 1992)

Guide to Eastern Germany by Stephen Banister and Chris Patrick (Bradt updated 1991)

Hiking Guide to Romania by Tim Burford (Bradt 1993)

INDEX